MYRON STAGMAN

The Shakespeare-in-Essence Series

THE ADVENTURES OF FALSTAFF

City-State Press

Shakespeare-in-Essence: The Adventures of Falstaff

City-State Press
ISBN 0-9709265-9-6

About the Author

Dr. Myron Stagman, an American from Chicago and later San Francisco, was fascinated with Classical Greece since elementary school when reading of Marathon and Thermopylae, Pericles and Socrates, and especially about Athens' fabled Democracy. With a doctorate in English Literature, he became a Shakespearean scholar and a research scholar as well in the Greek Classics.

His often-stated goal: to communicate the essence of the Shakespearean and Greek classics to a general audience, to foster an understanding and appreciation of this wonderful heritage.

Other Works by the Author:

100 Prophecies of the Delphic Oracle
[Prophetic Advice from the God Apollo]

The prophecies, aside from their mystery and marvel, offer an ideal opportunity to describe the extraordinary culture and history of Ancient Greece.

The Athenian Acropolis
&
its Golden Age Background

The Acropolis is not simply monuments. It reflects the magnificent civilization of Classical Athens, its cultural achievements, personalities, living history.

Socrates, the Martyred Messiah
[An Essential History of Classical Athens]

A history of Athens during its Classical Age integrates the life and death of the moral philosopher Socrates, with original research casting light on the true causes of Socrates' martyrdom.

The Burlesque Comedies of Aristophanes

5 essays on Classical Athens (on Democracy, Slavery, Sex, God, and War) provide vital background information to blow-by-blow descriptions of the eleven surviving bawdy, cutting, ultra-democratic plays of the comedy genius.

The **Shakespeare-in-Essence** Series:
*The essence of the dialogue interpersed
with brief comments for comprehension
of Shakespeare's deeper meanings*
Shakespeare-in-Essence: *Four Monumental Tragedies*
Shakespeare-in-Essence: *Three Tragedies of Love*
Shakespeare-in-Essence: *Seven Comedies About Love*

Guide to Shakespeare
An introduction to all of Shakespeare's plays:
brief narrations of the story, highlights,
deeper meanings

Guide to Greek Drama
An introduction to all 44 surviving tragedies
and comedies of Classical Athens:
includes Aeschylus' *Prometheus Bound*
Sophocles' *Oedipus Rex*
Euripides' *Medea*
Aristophanes' *Clouds*

Shakespeare's Greek Drama Secret
The revelation of Shakespeare's mastery of Greek Drama
discloses for the first time this decisive influence on his
work.

Shakespeare-in-Essence: The Adventures of Falstaff

TABLE OF CONTENTS

Shakespeare-in-Essence: The Adventures of Falstaff

INTRODUCTION

Who is Falstaff? The greatest comic figure in Literature.

Who is Falstaff? An ever-humorous and witty, irreverent, impudent, artful dodging, shrewd, gluttonous, drinking ("sack", his trademark), whoremongering, manipulating and swindling (addicted to receiving loans he never gets around to paying back), rascal and humbug of enormous vitality (when roused to some unsavory action after sleeping late into the day after a late-night debauch) not to mention moral effrontery, utterly free of conventional ties and values, an aging rogue who quotes scripture in his mock-serious pretensions to an uneasy conscience and professions to reform.

In short, an enemy of heroism, honor, and simple decency, whom nearly everybody (except the censorious) becomes fond of, perhaps even (or especially) when he overreaches himself.

Shakespeare-in-Essence: The Adventures of Falstaff

Henry IV, Part I

The historical epic of
Honor versus Falstaff

Shakespeare-in-Essence: The Adventures of Falstaff

Henry IV, Part I

This chronicle play is one of Shakespeare's finest works, thanks largely to Falstaff, the (I say it again) greatest comic character in Literature. Hotspur, the brilliant rebel, wins our sympathy and centuries of admiring applause. Prince Henry, alias Hal, completes the triumverate of splendid characters in this epic of rebellion and counter-insurgency, of heroism and anti-heroism.

Act I, scene 1. London: the Palace. Rebellion has broken out against King Henry IV, the former Bolingbroke who usurped the throne of King Richard, and murdered him.

> *King.* So shaken as we are, so wan with care,
>   Find we a time for frighted peace to pant,
>   And breathe short-winded accents of new broils
>   To be commenced in strands afar remote.

They have suffered a dreadful loss to the Welshman, "wild Glendower". Welcome news, however, is that Henry Percy – Hotspur, the gallant son of Northumberland – has achieved a victory against enemy Scotsmen including the famed warrior, the Earl of Douglas. Hotspur has taken many prisoners who can be held for ransom.

The Earl of Westmoreland comments on Hotspur's exploit:

> A conquest for a prince to boast of.

The word "prince" reminds the King of his own son, Prince Henry, who has been anything but warlike in recent times.

> *King.* Yea, there thou mak'st me sad, and mak'st me sin
>   In envy, that my Lord Northumberland

Should be the father to so blest a son. --
A son who is the theme of honor's tongue,
Amongst a grove the very straightest plant,
Who is sweet Fortune's minion and her pride,
While I by looking on the praise of him
See riot and dishonor stain the brow
Of my young Harry.

O that it could be proved
That some night-tripping fairy had exchanged
In cradle-clothes our children where they lay,
And called mine Percy, his Plantagenet,
Then would I have his Harry, and he mine.

I.2.   London. The Prince's lodging. Enter Prince Henry –
Hal – to awaken the late-slumbering Sir John Falstaff,
snoring upon a bench in a corner.

Falstaff.   Now, Hal, what time of day is it, lad?

That was the first line of perhaps the most extraordinary and
humorous and surely the most corpulent (*Prince.* "How
long is't ago, Jack, since thou sawest thine own knee?") and
outrageous fellow to cross a stage or printed page, the
utterly incomparable Falstaff. He and Prince Hal have been
setting records in dissipation, "riot and dishonor" (to quote
the King).

Prince.   Thou art so fat-witted with drinking of old
sack [a Spanish white wine, a drink associated with
Falstaff], and unbuttoning thee after supper, and
sleeping upon benches after noon, that thou hast
forgotten to demand that truly which thou wouldst

14

truly know. What a devil hast thou to do with the time of the day? Unless hours were cups of sack, and minutes capons, and clocks the tongues of bawds, and dials the signs of leaping-houses [brothels], and the blessed sun himself a fair hot wench in flame-colored taffeta, I see no reason why thou shouldst be so superfluous to demand the time of the day.

That pretty well sums up Falstaff's life-style – drinking, gluttonising, whoring, sleeping. And he in his 50's.

Falstaff. Indeed, you come near me now, Hal, for we that take purses go by the moon and the seven stars, and not by Phoebus [the sun], he, 'that wandering knight so fair'.

Yes, they also "take purses", engaging in the sport of robbery to pay for all this fun.

Falstaff. Is not my hostess of the tavern a most sweet wench?

Prince. Is not a buff jerkin a most sweet robe of durance?

["durance": a play on "durable" and "confinement", as a buff jerkin was a leather jacket of yellow hue worn customarily by sheriffs.]

Falstaff. How now, how now mad wag? What a plague have I to do with a buff jerkin?

Prince. Why, what a pox have I to do with my hostess of the tavern?

Falstaff. Well, thou hast called her to a reckoning

15

[the bill, and maybe a sexual tryst as well]
many a time and oft.

Prince.   Did I ever call for thee to pay thy part?

Falstaff. No, I'll give thee thy due, thou hast
paid all there.

Prince.   Yea and elsewhere, so far as my coin would
stretch, and where it would not, I have used my
credit.

Probably more than money is meant here. Hal uses his credit
– position – to keep Falstaff away from that buff jerkin.

Falstaff.   Yea, and so used it that were it not here
apparent that thou art heir apparent – but I prithee
sweet wag, shall there be gallows standing in
England when thou art King? Do not thou when
thou art King hang a thief.

Prince.   No, thou shalt.

Falstaff. Shall I? O rare! By the Lord I'll be a
brave judge.

Prince.   Thou judgest false already. I mean thou shalt
have the hanging of the thieves, and so become a
rare hangman.

Hal means rare as both "fine" (as Falstaff had just used the
word) and "rare", meaning it is rare for a highwayman to
hang other thieves!

Falstaff.   Thou hast done much harm upon me Hal,
God forgive thee for it. Before I knew thee Hal,
I knew nothing [was innocent, naïve], and now
am I, if a man should speak truly, little more than

16

one of the wicked.

I must give over this life, and I will give it over.
By the Lord an [if] I do not, I am a villain. I'll
be damned for never a king's son in Christendom.

Prince. Where shall we take a purse tomorrow Jack?

Falstaff. Zounds ["by God's wounds"],
where thou wilt lad. I'll make one [count me in];
an I do not, call me villain and baffle me.

In those days "baffling" purported hanging by the heels or
other such public chastisement and humiliation.

Prince. I see a good amendment of life in thee,
from praying to purse-taking.

Falstaff. Why Hal, 'tis my vocation, Hal.
'Tis no sin for a man to labor in his vocation.

Enter Poins

Poins is a gentleman crony of theirs, another who goes "by
the moon" for fun and profit.

Falstaff. Poins! Now shall we know if Gadshill
have set a match. [Gadshill is their "setter", he
who "cases the joint", supplies information,
setting up the robbery.] O if men were to be saved
by merit, what hole in hell were hot enough for
him? This is the most omnipotent villain that ever
cried Stand to a true man.

[merit: concerning the theological doctrine of salvation by
works (versus salvation by faith). "Stand" = halt, to a "true"
= honest man.]

17

Prince.   Good morrow Ned.

Poins.   Good morrow sweet Hal. What says Sir
John Sack-and-Sugar? Jack, how agrees the
devil and thee about thy soul that thou soldest
him on Good Friday last, for a cup of Madeira
and a cold capon's leg?

But my lads, my lads, tomorrow morning, by four
o'clock early at Gad's Hill [a hill on the main
road from London; their setter was nicknamed
"Gadshill" due to his frequent reconnaissances
in this notorious region], there are pilgrims
going to Canterbury with rich offerings, and
traders riding to London with fat purses.

I have vizards [masks] for you all. You have
horses for yourselves. Gadshill lies [their
setter lodges] tonight in Rochester [near that
strategic hill]. We may do it as secure as sleep.
If you will go I will stuff your purses full of
crowns. If you will not, tarry at home and be
hanged.

Falstaff.   If I tarry at home and go not, I'll hang
you for going. Hal, wilt thou make one?

Prince.   Who, I rob? I a thief? Not I by my faith.

Falstaff.   There's neither honesty, manhood,
nor good fellowship in thee.

Prince.   Well then, once in my days I'll be a madcap.

Falstaff.   Why, that's well said.

Prince.   Well, come what will, I'll tarry at home.

Falstaff. By the Lord, I'll be a traitor then,
when thou art King.

Poins. Sir John, I prithee leave the Prince and me
alone. I will lay him down such reasons for this
adventure that he shall go.

Falstaff. Well, God give thee the spirit of
persuasion, and him the ears of profiting.
Farewell, you shall find me in Eastcheap.

Falstaff departs for their hangout, the Boar's Head Tavern
in a slummy part of London, Eastcheap.

Poins. Now, my good sweet honey lord, ride with us
tomorrow. I have a jest to execute that I cannot
manage alone. Falstaff, Bardolph, Peto, and
Gadshill shall rob those men that we have already
waylaid [planned to rob]. Yourself and I will not
be there; and when they have the booty, if you and
I do not rob them, cut this head off from my
shoulders.

Prince. But how shall we part with them in setting
forth?

Poins. Why, we will set forth before or after them,
and appoint them a place of meeting, wherein it is
at our pleasure to fail. And then they will adventure
upon the exploit themselves, which they shall have
no sooner achieved but we'll set upon them.

Prince. Yea but 'tis like they will know us by our
horses, by our habits [clothes], and by every other
appointment, to be ourselves.

Poins. Tut, our horses they shall not see; I'll tie them

19

in the wood. Our vizards we will change after we
leave them; and sirrah, I have cases of buckram
[a type of coarse cloth they will dress in] for the
nonce, to inmask our noted outward garments.

Prince.   Yea, but I doubt they will be too hard for us.

Poins.   Well, for two of them, I know them to be as
true-bred cowards as ever turned back. And for
the third [Falstaff], if he fight longer than he sees
reason, I'll forswear arms.

The virtue of this jest will be the incomprehensible
lies that this same fat rogue will tell us when we
meet at supper, how thirty at least he fought with,
what wards [warding off, parrying of thrusts],
what blows, what extremities he endured, and in
the reproof of this lives the jest.

Prince.   Well, I'll go with thee. Provide us all things
necessary, and meet me tonight in Eastcheap;
there I'll sup. Farewell.

Poins.   Farewell, my lord.   [*exit*

Alone, the Prince reveals another disposition.

Prince Henry.   I know you all, and will a while uphold
The unyoked humor of your idleness.
Yet herein will I imitate the sun
[the sun was an emblem of royalty]
Who doth permit the base contagious clouds
To smother up his beauty from the world,
That when he please again to be himself,
Being wanted he may be more wondered at
By breaking through the foul and ugly mists,

Of vapors that did seem to strangle him.

So when this loose behavior I throw off,
And pay that debt I never promised,
By how much better than my word I am,
By so much shall I falsify men's hopes
   [expectations],
And like bright metal on a sullen ground,
My reformation glittering o'er my fault,
Shall show more goodly, and attract more eyes,
Than that which hath no foil to set it off.

I'll so offend, to make offence a skill,
Redeeming time when men think least I will.

                           [*exit*

Hal unmasks his purpose to reform and redeem himself.
His words and tone indicate he means it. And this speech
was delivered in **poetry**, not the prose in which his previous
talk and jests were spoken.

1.3 Windsor: the Castle. King Henry, his supporter Lord
Blunt, others, and Northumberland, his son Hotspur, and
Worcester. The latter three lords were instrumental in aiding
Bolingbroke to overthrow King Richard II and become
King.

   King.   My blood hath been too cold and temperate,
          Unapt to stir at these indignities,
          And you have found me, for accordingly
          You tread upon my patience. But be sure
          I will from henceforth rather be myself,
          Mighty and to be feared, than my condition,

> Which hath been smooth as oil, soft as young down,
> And therefore lost that title of respect
> Which the proud soul ne'er pays but to the proud.

Worcester. Our house, my sovereign liege, little deserves
> The scourge of greatness to be used on it,
> And that same greatness too which our own hands
> Have holp to make so portly.

King.   Worcester, get thee gone, for I do see
> Danger and disobedience in thine eye.
> When we need
> Your advice and counsel, we shall send for you.
>   [*Worcester goes out*

Northumberland.   Yea, my good lord.
> Those prisoners in your highness' name demanded,
> Which Harry Percy [his son Hotspur] here at
>   Holmedon took,
> Were, as he says, not with such strength denied
> As is delivered to your majesty.
> Either envy, therefore, or misprision
> Is guilty of this fault, and not my son.

Hotspur now speaks, double-talking the King in his own colorful fashion of explanation:

Hotspur.   My liege, I did deny no prisoners.
> But I remember, when the fight was done,
> When I was dry with rage and extreme toil,
> Breathless and faint, leaning upon my sword,
> Came there a certain lord, neat and trimly dressed,
> Fresh as a bridegroom, and his chin new reaped
> Showed like a stubble-land at harvest-home.
> He was perfumed like a milliner,

And 'twixt his finger and his thumb he held
A pouncet-box, which ever and anon
He gave his nose and took't away again –
Who, therewith angry, when it next came there,
Took it in snuff – and still he smiled and talked.
And as the soldiers bore dead bodies by,
He called them untaught knaves, unmannerly,
To bring a slovenly unhandsome corse [corpse]
Betwixt the wind and his nobility.

Hotspur truly has imagination and personality to go with his swashbuckling exploits on the battlefield.

With many holiday and lady terms
He questioned me, amongst the rest demanded
My prisoners in your majesty's behalf.
I then, all smarting with my wounds being cold,
To be so pestered with a popinjay,
Out of my grief and my impatience,
Answered neglectingly I know not what,
He should, or he should not, for he made me mad
To see him shine so brisk, and smell so sweet,
And talk so like a waiting-gentlewoman
Of guns, and drums, and wounds.

In sum,

I answered indirectly as I said,
And I beseech you, let not his report
Come current for an accusation
Betwixt my love and your high majesty.

Lord Blunt seeks to mediate: whatever may have happened, it matters not, "so he unsay it now".

King. Why, yet he doth deny his prisoners,

23

But with proviso and exception,
That we at our own charge shall ransom straight
His brother-in-law, the foolish Mortimer,
Who, on my soul, hath wilfully betrayed
The lives of those that he did lead to fight
Against the great magician, damned Glendower,
Whose daughter, as we hear, that Earl of March
  [Mortimer]
Hath lately married.

Shall our coffers then
Be emptied to redeem a traitor home?
Shall we buy treason?

Hotspur. He never did fall off, my sovereign liege,
But by the chance of war. To prove that true
Needs no more but one tongue for all those wounds,
Those mouthed wounds, which valiantly he took,
When on the gentle Severn's sedgy bank,
In single opposition, hand to hand,
He did confound the best part of an hour
In changing hardiment with great Glendower.

King. Thou dost belie him, Percy, thou dost belie him.
He never did encounter with Glendower.
I tell thee,
He durst as well have met the devil alone,
As Owen Glendower for an enemy.

Let me not hear you speak of Mortimer.
Send me your prisoners with the speediest means,
Or you shall hear in such a kind from me
As will displease you.

King Henry, Blunt and others leave the chamber. Hotspur remains with his father Northumberland.

Hotspur. An if the devil come and roar them,
I will not send them. I will after straight
And tell him so, for I will ease my heart,
Albeit I make a hazard of my head.

Northumberland. What, drunk with choler? Stay and
pause awhile.
Here comes your uncle.

Northumberland is much more cautious and controlled than his son.

Worcester returns

Hotspur. Speak of Mortimer!
Zounds, I will speak of him, and let my soul
Want mercy if I do not join with him.
Yea, on his part, I'll empty all these veins,
And shed my dear blood drop by drop in the dust,
But I will lift the down-trod Mortimer
As high in the air as this unthankful king,
As this ingrate and cank'red Bolingbroke.

Worcester explains that Mortimer was proclaimed heir to the throne by King Richard before he set forth on his Irish expedition. Hotspur and Northumberland now understand that King Henry has a strong reason to want Mortimer dead.

Hotspur denounces Henry again as treacherous and disdainful, an ingrate whom they helped lift to the throne, which included the murder of King Richard. We have been "forced, discarded, and shook off by him", and he insists they redeem themselves and their honor by openly opposing "this proud king". The fiery Hotspur soars in his rhetoric as he does in his martial deeds:

> By heaven, methinks it were an easy leap,
> To pluck bright honor from the pale-faced moon,
> Or dive into the bottom of the deep,
> Where fathom-line could never touch the ground,
> And pluck up drowned honor by the locks,
> So he that doth redeem her thence might wear
> Without corrival [partner] all her dignities.

More down-to-earth, regarding the Scottish prisoners,

> I'll keep them all.
> By God, he shall not have a Scot of them.

Hotspur cannot leave off, cannot forget perceived injustices by the King, "this vile politician, Bolingbroke". (I must say, that is a blunt and acute judgment.) He remembers, "what a candy deal of courtesy this fawning greyhound then did proffer me!"

> *Worcester.* The King will always think him in our debt,
> And think we think ourselves unsatisfied,
> Till he hath found a time to pay us home.
> And see already how he doth begin
> To make us strangers to his looks of love.

They begin to organize their forces for revolt. The first step: they will free the Scottish prisoners without ransom and ally themselves with Douglas, a formidable fighting Scotsman.

Hotspur concludes the First Act:

> Uncle, adieu. O, let the hours be short,
> Till fields, and blows, and groans applaud
> our sport!

26

Act II, scene 1.   Rochester, an inn yard.   The "setter",
Gadshill, converses with one of his sources of information.
The fellow questions Gadshill's ability to stay out of reach
of the hangman.

> *Gadshill.*   Tut! there are other Trojans that thou
> dream'st not of, the which for sport sake
> are content to do the profession some grace,

[The word "grace" alone, if one recalls a speech by Falstaff
on salvation, would indicate those the setter refers to.]

> that would, if matters should be looked into,
> for their own credit sake make all whole.
> I am joined with no foot-land-rakers,
> no long-staff sixpenny strikers, none of these
> mad mustachio purple-hued malt-worms, but with
> nobility and tranquillity, burgomasters and great
> onyers, such as can hold in, such as will strike
> sooner than speak, and speak sooner than drink,
> and drink sooner than pray. [Falstaff and Poins
> are of the "gentleman" class]
> And yet, zounds, I lie, for they pray con-
> tinually to their saint, the commonwealth, or
> rather not pray to her, but prey on her, for they
> ride up and down on her, and make her their boots.

II.2   A road near Gad's Hill, two miles from Rochester, at
night. Enter Hal and Poins, Peto and Bardolph. Poins runs
up to Hal, having played a trick on Falstaff by hiding his
horse.

> *Poins.* Come, shelter, shelter! I have removed Falstaff's

horse, and he frets like a gummed velvet.   [*he hides*

Falstaff (*entering breathless*).   Poins! Poins! And be
hanged! Poins!

Prince.   Peace, ye fat-kidneyed rascal! What a
brawling dost thou keep!

Falstaff.   Where's Poins, Hal?

Prince.   He is walked up to the top of the hill.
I'll go seek him.   [*he joins Poins in hiding*

Falstaff.   I am accursed to rob in that thief's company.
The rascal hath removed my horse, and tied him
I know not where. I doubt not but to die a fair
death for this, if I 'scape hanging for killing
that rogue. I have forsworn his company hourly
any time this two and twenty years, and yet I am
bewitched with the rogue's company. If the rascal
have not given me medicines to make me love him,
I'll be hanged.

Poins! Hal! a plague upon you both! Bardolph,
Peto! I'll starve ere I'll rob a foot further.
An 'twere not as good a deed as drink, to turn
true man and to leave these rogues, I am the
veriest varlet that ever chewed with a tooth.

Eight yards of uneven ground is threescore and
ten miles afoot with me, and the stony-hearted
villains know it well enough. A plague upon't
when thieves cannot be true one to another!
[*they whistle*] whew! – a plague upon you all!
Give me my horse, you rogues, give me my
horse and be hanged.

Prince (*coming forward*). Peace, ye fat-guts! Lie down, lay thine ear close to the ground and list if thou canst hear the tread of travellers.

Enter Gadshill, after which
Poins, Bardolph, and Peto come forward

Poins. O, 'tis our setter. I know his voice.

Bardolph. What news?.

Gadshill. Case ye, case ye, on with your vizards [masks], there's money of the King's coming down the hill, 'tis going to the King's exchequer.

Falstaff. You lie ye rogue, 'tis going to the King's tavern.

"King's tavern" was a nickname for any tavern, and Falstaff means he will divert the money to the tavern in which he drinks with the King's money.

Prince. Sirs, you four shall front them in the narrow lane. Ned Poins and I will walk lower [further down the road]. If they 'scape from your encounter, then they light on us.

Peto. How many be there of them?

Gadshill. Some eight or ten.

Falstaff. Zounds, will they not rob us?

Prince. What, a coward, Sir John Paunch?

Falstaff. Indeed I am not John of Gaunt your grandfather [that was indeed the name of the Prince's grandfather], but yet no coward, Hal.

Prince. Well, we leave that to the proof.

(*aside to Poins*) Ned, where are our disguises?

Poins (*aside to Hal*). Here, hard by, stand close.
[The disguises are nearby; let's drop out-of-sight.]

Hal and Poins leave Falstaff who has been informed by Poins where he can find his horse. Falstaff, Bardolph, Peto and Gadshill wait in ambush for the travellers while the Prince and Poins hide further down the hill. They are supposed to join Falstaff and the others immediately once the prey have arrived and been stopped by the four of them.

*Enter Well-Heeled Travellers,
on their way from London to Canterbury*

First Traveller. Come neighbor, the boy shall
lead our horses down the hill. We'll walk
afoot awhile and ease our legs.

Thieves. Stand!

Travellers. Jesus bless us!

Falstaff. Strike, down with them. Cut the villains'
throats. Ah, whoreson caterpillars, bacon-fed
knaves, they hate us youth[!]. Down with them,
fleece them.

Travellers. O we are undone, both we and ours
for ever.

Falstaff. Hang ye, gorbellied knaves, are ye undone?
No ye fat chuffs, I would your store were here.
On, bacons, on! What ye knaves, young men must
live.

30

The four bandits rob them and tie them up. At this point the scene shifts to Hal and Poins who have stayed away, donning disguises.

Prince. The thieves have bound the true men.
Now could thou and I rob the thieves, and go
merrily to London, it would be argument [a good
story], laughter for a month, and a good jest
for ever.

The bandits walk down the hill in the direction of Hal and Poins who are still in hiding. Then they stop and begin sharing the loot.

Re-enter Thieves

Falstaff. Come, my masters, let us share, and then
to horse before day. An the Prince and Poins
be not two arrant cowards, there's no equity stirring.
There's no more valor in that Poins than in a
wild duck.

Prince. Your money!

Poins. Villains!

Bardolph, Peto and Gadshill run away. Falstaff, after a blow or two, runs also, leaving the loot behind.

Prince. Got with much ease. Now merrily to horse.
The thieves are all scatterd, and possessed
with fear so strongly that they dare not meet
each other. Each takes his fellow for an officer.
Away, good Ned. Falstaff sweats to death, and
lards the lean earth as he walks along. Were't
not for laughing, I should pity him.

Poins. How the fat rogue roared!

II.3 A room in Warkworth Castle. Hotspur enters, reading a letter and pacing to and fro.

Hotspur.   "But, for mine own part, my lord, I could be
well contented to be there, in respect of the
love I bear your house."
He could be contented: why is he not then? In
respect of the love he bears our house: he shows
in this, he loves his own barn better than he loves
our house. Let me see some more.
"The purpose you undertake is dangerous."
Why, that's certain. 'Tis dangerous to take a cold,
to sleep, to drink, but I tell you, my lord fool,
out of the nettle, danger, we pluck this flower,
safety.
"The purpose you undertake is dangerous, the
friends you have named uncertain, the time
itself unsorted, and your whole plot too light
for the counterpoise of so great an opposition."
Say you so, say you so? What a lack-brain is this!
By the lord, our plot is a good plot as ever was
laid, our friends true and constant. . . . What a
frosty-spirited rogue is this! Zounds, an I were
now by this rascal, I could brain him with his
lady's fan. Is there not my father, my uncle, and
myself? Lord Edmund Mortimer, my lord of York,
and Owen Glendower? Is there not besides the
Douglas? Have I not all their letters to meet me

in arms by the ninth of the next month? and are
they not some of them set forward already?

Ha! You shall see now, in very sincerity of
fear and cold heart, will he to the King and lay
open all our proceedings! O, I could divide
myself and go to buffets, for moving such a dish
of skim milk with so honorable an action! Hang
him! let him tell the King: we are prepared. I will
set forward tonight.

Enter Lady Percy

How now, Kate? I must leave you within
these two hours.

Hotspur's wife Kate, lively and playful and a good match
for her husband, tries to find out what's going on. He jokes
with her and puts her off.

Lady Percy.   O my good lord, why are you thus alone?
For what offence have I this fortnight been
A banished woman from my Harry's bed?
Tell me, sweet lord, what is't that takes from thee
Thy stomach, pleasure, and thy golden sleep?
Why dost thou bend thine eyes upon the earth,
And start so often when thou sit'st alone?
Why hast thou lost the fresh blood in thy cheeks,
And given my treasures and my rights of thee
To thick-eyed musing and curst melancholy?

Kate says that Hotspur, in his slumbers, murmurs of sallies
and retires, trenches and tents, parapets and cannon, of
prisoners' ransom and soldiers slain.

O, what portents are these?

33

Some heavy business hath my lord in hand,
And I must know it, else he loves me not.

Hotspur (*calling for a servant*).   What, ho!
   Hath Butler brought those horses from the
      sheriff?

Servant.   One horse, my lord, he brought even now.

Hotspur.   What horse? a roan, a crop-ear, is it not?

Servant.   It is, my lord.

Hotspur.   That roan shall by my throne.

                           [*the servant goes*

Lady Percy.   But hear you, my lord.

Hotspur.   What say'st thou, my lady?

Lady Percy.   What is it carries you away?

Hotspur.   Why, my horse, my love, my horse.

Lady Percy.   Out, you mad-headed ape!
   A weasel hath not such a deal of spleen
   As you are tossed with. In faith,
   I'll know your business, Harry, that I will.
   I fear my brother Mortimer doth stir
   About his title, and hath sent for you
   To line his enterprise. But if you go --

Hotspur.   So far afoot, I shall be weary, love.

Lady Percy.   Come, come, you paraquito, answer me
   Directly unto this question that I ask.
   In faith, I'll break thy little finger, Harry,
   An if thou wilt not tell me all things true.

Hotspur.   Away, you trifler! Love! I love thee not,

34

I care not for thee, Kate. This is no world
To play with mammets and to tilt with lips.
We must have bloody noses and cracked crowns,
And pass them current too. God's me, my horse!
What say'st thou, Kate? What wouldst thou have
   with me?

Lady Percy. Do you not love me? do you not, indeed?
   Well, do not then, for since you love me not
   I will not love myself. Do you not love me?
   Nay, tell me if you speak in jest or no.

Hotspur. Come, wilt thou see me ride?
   And when I am a-horseback,
   I will swear I love thee infinitely.

   But hark you, Kate,
   I must not have you henceforth question me
   Whither I go, nor reason whereabout.
   Whither I must, I must. And, to conclude,
   This evening must I leave you, gentle Kate.
   I know you wise, but yet no farther wise
   Than Harry Percy's wife. Constant you are,
   But yet a woman, and for secrecy,
   No lady closer, for I well believe
   Thou wilt not utter what thou dost not know.
   And so far will I trust thee, gentle Kate!

Lady Percy. How! so far?

Hotspur. Not an inch further. But hark you, Kate,
   Whither I go, thither shall you go too.
   Today will I set forth, tomorrow you --
   Will this content you, Kate?

Lady Percy. It must, of force.

II.4   Eastcheap, the Boar's Head Tavern, at midnight. The first part of this scene involves the Prince in one room of the tavern, Poins in another, and the waiter Francis joshingly belabored by Hal while Poins – as per prior arrangement with Hal – keeps calling Francis to come over. The critics loathe this scene and consider the humor in poor taste. But it happens to be an allegorical skit in which the participants each symbolize someone or something. See if you can figure out **who** the Prince, Poins, and Francis are supposed to represent, **what** they are enacting, and **what** does Shakespeare intend the vintner (innkeeper) to stand for.

Prince.   Come hither, Francis.

Francis.   My lord?

Prince.   How long hast thou to serve, Francis?

Francis.   Forsooth, five years, and as much as to --

Poins (*within*).   Francis!

Francis.   Anon [in a moment], anon, sir.

Prince.   Five years! by'r lady, a long lease for the
          clinking of pewter. But, Francis, darest thou
          be so valiant as to play the coward with thy
          indenture and show it a fair pair of heels and
          run from it?

Francis.   O Lord, sir! I'll be sworn upon all the
          books in England. I could find in my heart --

Poins (*within*).   Francis!

Francis.   Anon, sir!

Prince.   How old art thou, Francis?

36

Francis. Let me see – about Michaelmas next I shall be --

Poins (within). Francis!

It goes on like this until the Prince and Poins simultaneously call Francis as he stands away from Hal. The stage direction has "Francis standing amazed, not knowing which way to go". Then the Vintner comes in:

Vintner. What! stand'st thou still, and hear'st such a calling. Look to the guests within.

[Francis goes

What does this mean? The answer lies in Hal's un-masking-speech. Francis, the fellow caught in-between, stands for Hal. The Prince, joking idly and incessantly, possessively, with Francis (i.e. with Hal), stands for Falstaff. Poins, calling Francis (i.e. calling the Prince) from a distance (that is, away at the palace), represents King Henry.

Therefore, the true set-up is Falstaff frivolously keeping Hal from going to King Henry and serving him.

The Vintner enters to decide matters for Francis (for the Prince). He sends him to Poins (to King Henry) where he belongs, doing his job. Who – or **what** – is the Vintner that tells Hal what he should be doing? Hal's **conscience**.

Back to literal reality, if that's what we have when Falstaff and his fellow robbers come in. Falstaff lambastes Hal and Poins for deserting them.

Falstaff. A plague of all cowards, I say, and a vengeance too! marry, and amen! Give me a cup of sack, boy. A plague of all cowards! Give me a cup of sack, rogue. Is there no

37

virtue extant?   [*he drinks*

Prince [joking about Falstaff perspiring and exhausted after his exertions]. Didst thou never see Titan [the sun] kiss a dish of butter that melted at the sweet tale of the sun's? If thou didst, then behold that compound.

Falstaff. Go thy ways, old Jack, die when thou wilt. If manhood, good manhood, be not forgot upon the face of the earth, then am I a shotten herring. There lives not three good men unhanged in England, and one of them is fat, and grows old. God help the while! a bad world, I say. A plague of all cowards, I say still.

Prince.   How now, wool-sack! what mutter you?

Falstaff.   A king's son!

Prince.   Why, you whoreson round man! what's the matter?

Falstaff. Are not you a coward? Answer me to that, and Poins there?

Poins.   Zounds, ye fat paunch, an ye call me coward, by the Lord I'll stab thee.

Falstaff.   I call thee coward? I'll see thee damned ere I call thee coward, but I would give a thousand pound I could run as fast as thou canst. You are straight enough in the shoulders, you care not who sees your back. Call you that **backing** of your friends? A plague upon such backing, give me them that will face me. Give me a cup of sack -- I am a rogue if I drunk today.

Prince.   O villain, thy lips are scarce wiped
  since thou drunk'st last.

Falstaff.   All's one for that. [*drinks*] A plague
  of all cowards still say I.

Prince.   What's the matter?

Falstaff.   What's the matter? There be four of us
  here have ta'en a thousand pound this day
  morning.

Prince.   Where is it, Jack, where is it?

Falstaff.   Where is it? Taken from us it is –
  a hundred upon poor four of us.

Prince.   What, a hundred, man?

Falstaff.   I am a rogue, if I were not at half-sword
  [close quarters] with a dozen of them two hours
  together. I have 'scaped by miracle. I am eight
  times thrust through the doublet, four through
  the hose [long stockings], my buckler [shield] cut
  through and through, my sword hacked like a
  hand-saw.

He goes on to say that he never fought better in his life, yet
even this was not enough against such odds. He continues
to berate his false "backers":

  A plague of all cowards. Let them the other three
  speak. If they speak more or less than truth,
  they are villains, and the sons of darkness.

Prince.   Speak sirs, how was it?

Gadshill.   We four set upon some dozen --

39

Falstaff. Sixteen at least, my lord.

Gadshill. And bound them. As we were sharing,
some six or seven fresh men set upon us --

Falstaff. And unbound the rest, and then come in the
other [another, new group of assailants].

Prince. What, fought you with them all?

Falstaff. All? I know not what you call all,
but if I fought not with fifty of them I am
a bunch of radish. If there were not two or
three and fifty upon poor old Jack, then am
I no two-legged creature.

Prince. Pray God you have not murdered some
of them.

Falstaff. Nay, that's past praying for. I have
peppered two of them. Two I am sure I have paid,
two rogues in buckram suits.
I tell thee what Hal, if I tell thee a lie,
spit in my face, call me horse. Thou knowest
my old ward defensive stance; here I lay,
and thus I bore my point. Four rogues in
buckram let drive at me --

Prince. What, four? Thou saidst but two even now.

Falstaff. Four, Hal, I told thee four.

Poins. Ay, ay, he said four.

Falstaff. These four came all a-front, and mainly
thrust at me. I made me no more ado, but
took all their seven points in my targets, thus.

Prince. Seven? Why, there were but four even now.

40

Falstaff. In buckram?

Poins. Ay, four, in buckram suits.

The story goes on, until Falstaff recounts how "seven of the eleven I paid". By "paid" we are led to believe he wounded them sorely, probably fatally.

Prince. O monstrous! Eleven buckram men
grown out of two.

Falstaff. But as the devil would have it, three
misbegotten knaves in Kendal green came
at my back, and let drive at me, for it was so
dark Hal, that thou couldst not see thy hand.

Prince. These lies are like their father that begets
them, gross as a mountain, open, palpable.
Why, thou clay-brained guts, thou knotty-pated
fool, thou whoreson, obscene, greasy
tallow-catch --

Falstaff. What, art thou mad? art thou mad?
Is not the truth the truth?

Prince. Why, how couldst thou know these men in
Kendal green when it was so dark thou couldst
not see thy hand? come tell us your reason.
What sayest thou to this?

Poins. Come, your reason Jack, your reason.

Falstaff. What, upon compulsion? Zounds,
an I were at the strappado [a type of torture],
or all the racks in the world, I would not tell
you on compulsion. If reasons were as plentiful
as blackberries, I would give no man a reason

upon compulsion.

Prince. I'll be no longer guilty of this sin;
this sanguine coward, this bed-presser, this
horseback-breaker, this huge hill of flesh--

Falstaff. 'Sblood [God's blood] you starveling,-
You eel-skin, you bull's pizzle,

and other Renaissance terms berating Hal's thinness (in
contrast to Hal's terminology delineating Falstaff).

Prince. When thou hast tired thyself in base
comparisons, hear me speak but this.

Poins. Mark, Jack.

Prince. We two saw you four set on four, and
bound them and were masters of their wealth.
Mark now how a plain tale shall put you down.
Then did we two set on you four, and with a
word, out-faced you from your prize, and have
it, yea, and can show it you here in the house.

And Falstaff, you carried your guts away as nimbly,
with as quick dexterity, and roared for mercy, and
still run and roared, as ever I heard bull-calf.

What a slave art thou to hack thy sword as thou
hast done, and then say it was in fight!

Could Falstaff really have done that? Would any warrior?

What trick, what device, what starting-hole
[a hole in which small animals would dive into
for safety] canst thou now find out, to hide
thee from this open and apparent shame?

Poins. Come, let's hear Jack, what trick hast
thou now?

Falstaff. By the Lord, I knew ye as well as he
that made ye. Why hear you my masters, was it
for me to kill the heir apparent? Should I turn
upon the true Prince? Why, thou knowest I am as
valiant as Hercules; but beware instinct, the lion
will not touch the true Prince.

Instinct is a great matter. I was now a coward on
instinct. I shall think the better of myself, and
thee, during my life; I for a valliant lion, and thou
for a true Prince.

But by the Lord, lads, I am glad you have the money.
Gallants, lads, boys, hearts of gold, all the titles
of good fellowship come to you.
What, shall we be merry, shall we have a play
extempore?

Taverns in the English Renaissance witnessed many impro-
vised little plays, such was the acute nature of people in those
days. Along this line, it is interesting to note that many
common folk who would be deemed quite illiterate could sit
in the penny-a-ticket seats at Shakespeare's plays and quite
understand the dramatic poetry being spoken.

Prince. Content, and the argument [story] shall be
thy running away.

Falstaff. Ah, no more of that Hal, an thou lovest me.

Enter Hostess

Hostess. O Jesu, my lord the Prince –

Prince. How now, my lady the hostess, what
  sayst thou to me?

Hostess. Marry my lord, there is a nobleman
  of the Court at door would speak with you.
  He says he comes from your father.

Hal prefers to play, but has Falstaff go out to talk with him.
With Falstaff gone, the Prince has Peto and Bardolph
explain about Falstaff's hacked-up sword and all of their
pretensions to having taken part in a whale-of-a-battle.
  The great pretender returns.

Falstaff. There's villainous news abroad.
  Here was Sir John Bracy from your father.

The news portends a looming civil war, with notables rising
against the King. They include the magnate Northumberland
and his brilliantly martial son Hotspur, the renowned
Glendower from Wales and his son-in-law (of English royal
blood) Mortimer, and the formidable fighting Scotsman
Douglas.

Falstaff. But tell me, Hal, art thou not horrible
  afeard? Thou being heir apparent, could the
  world pick thee out three such enemies again
  as that fiend Douglas, that spirit Percy [demon
  Hotspur], and that devil Glendower? Doth not
  thy blood thrill at it?

Prince. Not a whit i' faith, I lack some of thy
  instinct.

Falstaff. Well, thou wilt be horribly chid
  tomorrow when thou comest to thy father.
  If thou love me, practice an answer.

Prince. Do thou stand for my father and examine
me upon the particulars of my life.

Falstaff. Shall I? Content. This chair shall be my
state [throne], this dagger my sceptre, and this
cushion my crown.
Give me a cup of sack to make my eyes look red,
that it may be thought I have wept; for I must
speak in passion.

Prince [bending his leg as if bowing before the King].
Well, here is my leg.

Falstaff. And here is my speech. Stand aside,
nobility.

Hostess. O Jesu, this is excellent sport i' faith.

Falstaff. Harry, I do not only marvel where thou
spendest thy time, but also how thou art
accompanied.

That thou art my son I have partly thy mother's
word, partly my own opinion, but chiefly a
villainous trick of thine eye, and a foolish
hanging of thy nether lip, that doth warrant me.
If then thou be son to me, here lies the point –
why, being son to me, art thou so pointed at?

Shall the son of England prove a thief, and take
purses? A question to be asked. There is a thing,
Harry, which thou hast often heard of, and it is
known to many in our land by the name of pitch.
This pitch, as ancient writers do report, doth
defile, so doth the company thou keepest.

And yet there is a virtuous man, whom I have

45

often noted in thy company, but I know not
his name.

Prince. What manner of man, an it like your Majesty?

Falstaff. A good portly man i' faith, and a corpulent,
of a cheerful look, a pleasing eye, and a most
noble carriage, and as I think, his age some
fifty, or by'r lady inclining to threescore. And
now I remember me, his name is Falstaff. If that
man should be lewdly given, he deceiveth me; for
Harry, I see virtue in his looks.

There is virtue in that Falstaff; him keep with,
the rest banish. And tell me now, thou naughty
varlet, tell me where hast thou been this month?

Prince. Dost thou speak like a king? Do thou stand
for me, and I'll play my father.

Falstaff. Depose me? If thou dost it half so gravely,
so majestically, both in word and matter, hang me
up by the heels for a rabbit-sucker, or a poulter's
hare.

Prince. Well, here I am set.
Now, Harry, whence come you?

Falstaff. My noble lord, from Eastcheap.

Prince. The complaints I hear of thee are grievous.

Falstaff. 'Sblood, my lord, they are false.

Prince. Thou art violently carried away from grace.
There is a devil haunts thee in the likeness
of an old fat man. Why dost thou converse with
that trunk of humors . . . that reverend vice,

that grey iniquity, that father ruffian, that
vanity in years? wherein villainous, but in all
things? wherein worthy, but in nothing?

Falstaff. I would your grace would take me with you.
Whom means your grace?

Prince. That villainous abominable misleader of
youth, Falstaff, that old white-bearded Satan.

Falstaff. No, my good lord – banish Peto, banish
Bardolph, banish Poins, but for sweet Jack
Falstaff, kind Jack Falstaff, true Jack Falstaff,
valiant Jack Falstaff, and therefore more valiant
being as he is old Jack Falstaff, banish not him
thy Harry's company. Banish plump Jack, and
banish all the world.

Prince. I do, I will.

Enter Bardolph, running

Bardolph bursts in with news that "the sheriff with a most
monstrous watch is at the door!" Falstaff wants to finish the
play, "I have much to say in the behalf of that Falstaff."
But this is serious. The sheriff has come to search for "a
gross fat man" who has committed a robbery. The Prince
tells Falstaff to hide, and uses his rank to get rid of the sheriff.

Act III, scene 1. In Wales, in Glendower's house,
Hotspur, Mortimer, Worcester, and Owen Glendower enter
into a pact to join forces against King Henry. Glendower's
an interesting, impressive man. Hotspur baits his supposed

supernatural powers, but the Welshman has self-control to go with his prowess and personality.

Glendower. At my nativity
> The front of heaven was full of fiery shapes,
> Of burning cressets, and at my birth
> The frame and huge foundation of the earth
> Shaked like a coward.

Hotspur. Why, so it would have been at the same
> season, if your mother's cat had but kittened,
> though yourself had never been born.

Glendower. I say the earth did shake when I was born.

Hotspur. And I say the earth was not of my mind,
> If you suppose as fearing you it shook.

Glendower. Cousin, of many men
> I do not bear these crossings.
> These signs have marked me extraordinary,
> And all the courses of my life do show
> I am not in the common roll of men.

Hotspur. I think there's no man speaks better Welsh.
> I'll to dinner.   [*he rises*

Mortimer (*alone to Hotspur*). Peace, cousin Percy,
> you will make him mad.

Glendower. I can call spirits from the vasty deep.

Hotspur. Why, so can I, or so can any man,
> Bul will they come when you do call for them?

Mortimer [who is a relation of Hotspur's, and
> Glendower's son-in-law, has a claim to the throne
> of England, and does not want to see allies and

family members crossing one another]. Come,
come, no more of this unprofitable chat.

Glendower.   Three times hath Henry Bolingbroke made
  head
  Against my power--thrice from the banks of Wye
  And sandy-bottomed Severn have I sent him
  Bootless home and weather-beaten back.

Hotspur.   Home without boots, and in foul weather too!
  How 'scapes he agues, in the devil's name?

Glendower ignores this, and takes out a map to get down to
business.   Finished, he goes out and Mortimer rounds on
Hotspur.

Mortimer.   Fie, cousin Percy! how you cross my father!

Hotspur.   I cannot choose. Sometime he angers me
  With telling me of the moldwarp and the ant,
  Of the dreamer Merlin and his prophecies,
  And of a dragon and a finless fish. . . .
  I tell you what--
  He held me last night at least nine hours
  In reckoning up the several devil's names
  That were his lackeys.

Mortimer.   In faith, he is a worthy gentleman,
  Exceedingly well read, and profited
  In strange concealments, valiant as a lion,
  And wondrous affable; and as bountiful
  As mines of India.
  Shall I tell you cousin?
  He holds your temper in a high respect,
  [Hotspur's high-spirited temperament]

And curbs himself even of his natural scope
When you come 'cross his humor, faith he does.
I warrant you that man is not alive
Might so have tempted him as you have done,
Without the taste of danger and reproof.
But do not use it oft, let me entreat you.

Worcester.   In faith, my lord, you are too
    wilful-blame
And since your coming hither have done enough
To put him quite besides his patience.
You must needs learn, lord, to amend this fault.
Though sometimes it show greatness, courage, blood,
And that's the dearest grace it renders you.
Yet oftentimes it doth present harsh rage,
Defect of manners, want of government,
Pride, haughtiness, opinion [conceit], and disdain,
The least of which haunting a nobleman
Loseth men's hearts and leaves behind a stain
Upon the beauty of all parts besides,
Beguiling them of commendation.

Hotspur.   Well, I am schooled; good manners
    be you speed.

He sounds a little chastened, but also dubious about the influence of etiquette in grand designs. He finishes with,

Here come our wives, and let us take our leaves.

III.2   London: the palace. Enter King Henry, Prince Henry, and Lords.

King.   Lords, give us leave, the Prince of Wales and I

50

Must have some private conference; but be near
   at hand,
For we shall presently have need of you.

                            [exeunt Lords

Now the King turns to his son:

I know not whether God will have it so,
For some displeasing service I have done,
That in his secret doom, out of my blood
He'll breed revengement and a scourge for me.
But thou dost in thy passages of life
Make me believe that thou art only marked
For the hot vengeance and the rod of heaven,
To punish my mistreadings. Tell me else,
Could such inordinate and low desires,
Such poor, such bare, such lewd, such mean
   attempts [activities],
Such barren pleasures, rude society,
As thou art matched withal, and grafted to,
Accompany the greatness of thy blood,
And hold their level with thy princely heart?

The Prince's perhaps somewhat embarrassed reply is a mixture of confession, blaming his youth and asking indulgence for it, together with a claim that others may have exaggerated his misdoings for political reasons. The King is by no means satisfied with this speech, and mentions Hal's lost place in council because everyone has rightly lost respect for him. King Henry then proceeds to compare Hal with Richard II, whom he (when Bolingbroke) had overthrown (Richard was under the strong influence, as Shakespeare portrayed him, of useless favorites):

The skipping King, he ambled up and down

51

> With shallow jesters, and rash bavin [brushwood]
>   wits,
> Soon kindled, and soon burnt.

Like Richard, the King states, the Prince has lost his dignity
with vile associations and actions.

> *Prince.* I shall hereafter, my thrice-gracious lord,
>   Be more myself.

> *King.* For all the world,
>   As thou art to this hour was Richard then.

Contrasts Hotspur to his son:

> When I from France set foot at Ravenspurgh,
>   [where he landed by ship from France,
>   coming unlawfully out of the exile pronounced
>   by Richard]
> And even as I was then is Percy [Hotspur] now.
> Now by my sceptre, and my soul to boot,
> He hath more worthy interest to the state
> Than thou the shadow of succession.
> For of no right, nor color like to right,
> He doth fill fields with harness in the realm
>   [brings armies into the field]
> Turns head against the lion's jaws,
>   [lion: a symbol of the King]
> And being no more in debt to years than thou,
>   [Hal and Hotspur are about the same age.]
> Leads ancient lords and reverend bishops on
> To bloody battles and to bruising arms.

> What never-dying honor hath he got
> Against renowned Douglas!

52

Thrice hath this Hotspur, Mars in swathling
   clothes,
This infant warrior, in his enterprises
Discomfited great Douglas, ta'en him once,
Enlarged him and made a friend of him,
To fill the mouth of deep defiance up,
And shake the peace and safety of our throne.

The King lists his foes, and names his son "my nearest
and dearest enemy". Hal swears reformation and coming
redemption.

Prince. I will redeem all this on Percy's head,
   And in the closing of some glorious day
   Be bold to tell you that I am your son,
   When I will wear a garment all of blood,
   And stain my favors in a bloody mask,
   Which washed away shall scour my shame with it.
   And that shall be the day, whene'er it lights,
   That this same child of honor and renown,
   This gallant Hotspur, this all-praised knight,
   And your unthought-of Harry chance to meet.

I shall make this northern youth exchange
His glorious deeds for my indignities.
Percy is but my factor, good my lord,
To engross up glorious deeds on my behalf,
And I will call him to so strict account
That he shall render every glory up,
Yea, even the slightest worship of his time,
Or I will tear the reckoning from his heart.

This, in the name of God, I promise here,
The which if He be pleased I shall perform.

I do beseech your majesty may salve
The long-grown wounds of my intemperature.
If not, the end of life cancels all bands,
And I will die a hundred thousand deaths
Ere break the smallest parcel of this vow.

King. A hundred thousand rebels die in this --
Thou shalt have charge and sovereign trust herein.

III.3 Eastcheap. A room in the Boar's Head Tavern, early
morning. The Prince enters to inform Falstaff that he has
procured for him a commission to recruit and organize
troops.

Prince. The land is burning, Percy stands on high,
And either we or they must lower lie.   [*he leaves*

Falstaff. Rare words! brave world! Hostess,
my breakfast, come!

Act IV, scene 1.   The rebel camp, near Shrewsbury.
Hotspur, Worcester, and Douglas. Letters arrive with the
force of a blow: Hotspur's father, Northumberland, is
"grievious sick" and cannot bring his army. Sir Richard
Vernon enters with more news.

Vernon. The King himself in person is set forth,
Or hitherwards intended speedily,
With strong and mighty preparation.

Hotspur. He shall be welcome too. Where is his son,
The nimble-footed madcap Prince of Wales,
And his comrades, that daff'd the world aside,

And bid it pass?

Vernon. All furnished, all in arms;
  All plumed like estridges that wing the wind,
  Baited like eagles having lately bathed,
  Glittering in golden coats like images,
  As full of spirit as the month of May,
  And gorgeous as the sun at midsummer;
  Wanton as youthful goats, wild as young bulls.

  I saw young Harry with his beaver [helmet] on,
  His cuisses on his thighs, gallantly armed,
  Rise from the ground like feathered Mercury,
  And vaulted with such ease into his seat,
  As if an angel dropped down from the clouds,
  To turn and wind a fiery Pegasus,
  And witch the world with noble horsemanship.

Hotspur. No more, no more! Worse than the sun in
      March,
  This praise doth nourish agues. Let them come,
  They come like sacrifices in their trim,
  And to the fire-eyed maid of smoky war
  All hot and bleeding will we offer them.

  Come, let me taste my horse,
  Who is to bear me like a thunderbolt
  Against the bosom of the Prince of Wales.
  Harry to Harry shall, hot horse to horse,
  Meet and ne'er part till one drop down a corse.
  O, that Glendower were come!

Vernon. There is more news.
  He cannot draw his power this fourteen days.

Douglas. That's the worst tidings that I hear of yet.

Worcester. Ay, by my faith, that bears a frosty sound.

Hotspur. Come, let us take a muster speedily --
Doomsday is near -- die all, die merrily.

IV.2 A road near Coventry. Enter Falstaff, now a captain in the royal army, talking to one of his officers, Bardolph, the quartermaster. Falstaff has a pistol-case slung at his enormous belt.

> *Falstaff.* Get thee before to Coventry; fill me a bottle
> of sack.

> *Bardolph.* Will you give me money, captain?

Falstaff tells him to take it out of their expense-money, and to give a message to "my lieutenant Peto". (What a military unit!) Bardolph goes, and Falstaff describes to us the men under his command.

> *Falstaff (solo).* If I be not ashamed of my soldiers,
> I am a soused gurnet. [if this needs an explanation,
> a "soused gurnet" is a type of fish pickled in salt]
> I have misused the King's press [power of
> conscription] damnably. A mad fellow met me on
> the way, and told me I had unloaded all the gibbets
> and pressed the dead bodies.
> No eye hath seen such scarecrows.
> Indeed I had the most of them out of prison.
> There's not a shirt and a half in all my company.
> But that's all one; they'll find linen enough on
> every hedge.

Enter Prince Henry and Westmoreland

Prince. Tell me, Jack, whose fellows are these that
come after?

Falstaff. Mine, Hal, mine.

Prince. I did never see such pitiful rascals.

Falstaff. Tut, tut, good enough to toss, food for powder,
food for powder – they'll fill a pit as well as
better; tush, man, mortal men, mortal men.

Prince. Make haste. Percy is already in the field.

                                             [he goes

Westmoreland. He is, Sir John. I fear we shall stay
    too long.   *[he hurries forward*

Falstaff. Well,
    To the latter end of a fray and the beginning of a feast
    Fits a dull fighter and a keen guest.   *[he follows*

Act V, scene 1.   The King's camp near Shrewsbury. The
character of Falstaff acts as a wonderful foil to the Heroic
Code and almost all respectable conventional values. In our
epic, what hath he to do with patriotism, discipline and self-
sacrifice, duty and responsibility, not to mention the
disregard of personal safety in the pursuit of military glory?

    The reformed and now serious-and-responsible Prince
has just left him, and Falstaff openly philosophizes in
soliloquy:

    What is honor? a word. What is in that word
    honor? air. A trim reckoning! Who hath it? he

that died a-Wednesday. Doth he feel it? no.
Doth he hear it? no. 'Tis insensible then? yea,
to the dead. But will it not live with the living? no.
Why? Detraction will not suffer it. Therefore I'll
none of it. Honor is a mere scutcheon -- and so
ends my catechism.

V.2   The rebel camp near Shrewsbury. They prepare for
battle.

Hotspur.   O gentlemen, the time of life is short!
            To spend that shortness basely were too long,
            If life did ride upon a dial's point,
            Still ending at the arrival of an hour.
            An if we live, we live to tread on kings.
            If die, brave death, when princes die with us!
            Now, for our consciences, the arms are fair,
            When the intent of bearing them is just.

V.3   The battlefield at Shrewsbury. King Henry has
"many marching in his coats", wearing the same clothing so
the enemy cannot single him out. The warrior Douglas kills
a number of them, including Sir Walter Blunt.

Enter Falstaff

Falstaff.   Soft! who are you? Sir Walter Blunt--there's
            honor for you! here's no vanity.
               I have led my ragamuffins where they are peppered,
            there's not three of my hundred and fifty left alive,
            and they are for the town's end, to beg during life.

It is perhaps as much realism as cynicism that suggests Falstaff purposely led his ragamuffins into the-thick-of-it in order to pocket their pay.

Enter Prince Henry

Prince. What, stand'st thou idle here? Lend me thy sword.
　　Many a nobleman lies stark and stiff
　　Under the hoofs of vaunting enemies,
　　Whose deaths are yet unrevenged. I prithee,
　　Lend me thy sword.

Falstaff. O Hal, I prithee, give me leave to breathe
　　awhile. Turk Gregory never did such deeds in
　　arms as I have done this day.
　　I have paid Percy, I have made him sure.

Prince. He is, indeed, and living to kill thee.
　　I prithee, lend me thy sword.

Falstaff. Nay, before God, Hal, if Percy be alive,
　　thou get'st not my sword, but take my pistol
　　if thou wilt.

Prince. Give it me. What, is it in the case?

Falstaff. Ay, Hal, 'tis hot, 'tis hot. There's that
　　will sack a city.

The Prince draws out the "pistol", which turns out to be a bottle of sack.

Prince. What, is it a time to jest and dally now?

Hal throws the bottle at him, and goes.

Falstaff (*alone*). I like not such grinning honor as
　　Sir Walter Blunt hath. Give me life, which if

I can save, so; if not, honor comes unlook't for,
and there's an end.

V.4   Douglas encounters another dressed as the King.

Douglas. I am the Douglas, fatal to all those
That wear those colors on them. What art thou,
That counterfeit'st the person of a king?

King. The King himself, who, Douglas, grieves at heart
So many of his shadows thou hast met,
And not the very King.
Seeing thou fall'st on me so luckily
I will assay thee. So, defend thyself.

Douglas. I fear thou art another counterfeit,
And yet in faith thou bear'st thee like a king.

They fight, and Douglas endangers the King's life. Prince
Henry rushes up to intervene. He fights with Douglas and
the latter flees. Hal moves to assist on another part of the
field, and his father says to him,

Stay, and breathe awhile.
Thou hast redeemed thy lost opinion.

King Henry departs, and Hotspur himself comes up to
Prince Henry.

Hotspur. If I mistake not, thou art Henry Monmouth.

Prince. Thou speak'st as if I would deny my name.

Hotspur. My name is Harry Percy.

Prince. Why, then I see
A very valiant rebel of the name.

I am the Prince of Wales, and think not, Percy,
To share with me in glory any more.
Two stars keep not their motion in one sphere,
Nor can one England brook a double reign,
Of Henry Percy and the Prince of Wales.

Hotspur. Nor shall it, Harry, for the hour is come
To end the one of us.

Prince. All the budding honors on thy crest
I'll crop, to make a garland for my head.

Hotspur. I can no longer brook thy vanities.

They engage each other, sword to sword. Falstaff approaches and cheers the Prince on:

Well said, Hal! to it, Hal!

Then Douglas returns, attacking Falstaff who falls down as if he were dead. Douglas moves on.
Hotspur is wounded, and falls.

Hotspur. O, Harry, thou hast robbed me of my youth!
I better brook the loss of brittle life
Than those proud titles thou hast won of me.
They wound my thoughts worse than thy sword
my flesh.
But thought's the slave of life, and life time's fool,
And time that takes survey of all the world
Must have a stop.

Hotspur dies.

Prince. Fare thee well, great heart!
Ill-weaved ambition, how much art thou shrunk!
When that this body did contain a spirit,

A kingdom for it was too small a bound,
But now two paces of the vilest earth
Is room enough. This earth, that bears thee dead,
Bears not alive so stout a gentleman.

Let my favors hide thy mangled face.
[*he covers Hotspur's eyes with a plume from his helm*
And even in thy behalf I'll thank myself
For doing these fair rites of tenderness.
Adieu, and take thy praise with thee to heaven.
Thy ignominy sleep with thee in the grave,
But not remembered in thy epitaph.

The Prince now sees Falstaff lying on the ground.

What! old acquaintance! could not all this flesh
Keep on a little life? poor Jack, farewell.
I could have better spared a better man.

The Prince exits and Falstaff rises from the ground. He says,

The better part of valor is discretion.

Falstaff spots the corpse of Hotspur, walks over and stabs it in the thigh, then throws the body over his shoulder. Prince Henry and his brother John of Lancaster return to encounter him. Hal says to Falstaff,

Art thou alive?
Or is it phantasy that plays upon our eyesight?
I prithee, speak.

Falstaff. There is Percy!   [*throwing the body
                                    on the ground*
If your father will do me any honor, so.

If not, let him kill the next Percy himself.
I look to be either earl or duke, I can assure you.

Prince. Why, Percy I killed myself, and saw thee dead.

Falstaff. Didst thou? Lord, Lord how this world is
given to lying! I grant you I was down and out of
breath, and so was he, but we rose both at an instant,
and fought a long hour by Shrewsbury clock. If I
may be delivered, so. If not, let them that should
reward valor bear the sin upon their own heads.
I'll take it upon my death, I gave him this wound
in the thigh. If the man were alive, and would
deny it, zounds, I would make him eat a piece of
my sword.

Lancaster. This is the strangest tale that ever I heard.

Prince. This is the strangest fellow, brother John.
[*aside, to Falstaff*] For my part, if a lie may do
thee grace,
I'll gild it with the happiest terms I have.

Hal and his brother leave, "to see what friends are living,
who are dead".

Falstaff. I'll follow, as they say, for reward. He that
rewards me, God reward him! If I do grow great,
I'll grow less, for I'll purge, and leave sack,
and live cleanly as a nobleman should do.

He drags off the body. As for his parting words, I personally
believe only that he follows for reward.

V.5 The Prince pardons Douglas, "ransomless and free":

Shakespeare-in-Essence: The Adventures of Falstaff

> His valors shown upon crests today
> Have taught us how to cherish such high deeds,
> Even in the bosom of our adversaries.

The play ends with King Henry giving orders to march against Northumberland and Glendower.

There will be a *Henry IV, Part II*. We shall see Falstaff again, and he will do his measly share to quell the final stage of the rebellion against the government. You may find him a bit huffed up after his heroics at Shrewsbury, but modesty and decorum were never his long suit.

CONCLUSION

Here are a few reminders of Falstaff from this epic play, *Henry the Fourth, Part One*:

Prince. What a devil hast thou to do with the
time of the day? Unless hours were cups of sack,
and minutes capons, and clocks the tongues of
bawds, and dials the signs of leaping-houses
[brothels], and the blessed sun himself a fair
hot wench in flame-colored taffeta, I see no
reason why thou shouldst be so superfluous to
demand the time of the day.

Falstaff. I am a rogue, if I were not at half-sword
[close quarters] with a dozen of them two hours
together.

Falstaff. Rare words! brave world! Hostess,
my breakfast, come!

Falstaff. What is honor? a word. What is in that word
honor? air. A trim reckoning! Who hath it? he
that died a-Wednesday. Doth he feel it? no.
Doth he hear it? no. 'Tis insensible then? yea,
to the dead. But will it not live with the living? no.
Why? Detraction will not suffer it. Therefore I'll
none of it. Honor is a mere scutcheon -- and so
ends my catechism.

Falstaff. There is Percy! *[throwing the body
on the ground*
If your father will do me any honor, so.
If not, let him kill the next Percy himself.
I look to be either earl or duke, I can assu

Shakespeare-in-Essence: The Adventures of Falstaff

Henry IV, Part II

The return of Rebellion and Falstaff

Shakespeare-in-Essence: The Adventures of Falstaff

INDUCTION

Warkworth: before the Earl of Northumberland's castle.

Enter Rumor, painted full of tongues

Rumor.   Open your ears; for which of you will stop
The vent of hearing when loud Rumor speaks?
I, from the orient to the drooping west,
Making the wind my post-horse, still unfold
The acts commenced on this ball of earth.
Upon my tongues continual slanders ride,
The which in every language I pronounce,
Stuffing the ears of men with false reports.

Rumor is a pipe blown by surmises,
    jealousies, conjectures,
And of so easy and so plain a stop
That the blunt monster with uncounted heads,
The still-discordant wavering multitude,
    [changeable public opinion]
Can play upon it.

My office is
To noise abroad that Harry Monmouth fell
    [Prince Henry, who was born at Monmouth]
Under the wrath of noble Hotspur's sword,
And that the King before the Douglas' rage
Stooped his anointed head as low as death.

This have I rumored through the peasant towns
Between that royal field of Shrewsbury
And this worm-eaten hold of ragged stone,
Where Hotspur's father, old Northumberland,
Lies crafty-sick.

69

Northumberland pretended to be ill, leaving Hotspur to fight without the aid of his father's army.

Act I, scene 1.   The same location.   Enter Lord Bardolph (**not** Falstaff and Hal's crony).

> *Northumberland.* What news, Lord Bardolph?
>> The times are wild. Contention, like a horse
>> Full of high feeding, madly hath broke loose
>> And bears down all before him.

> *Lord Bardolph.*   Noble Earl,
>> I bring you certain news from Shrewsbury.

> *Northumberland.*   Good, an God will!

> *Lord Bardolph.*   As good as heart can wish.
>> The King is almost wounded to the death;
>> And, in the fortune of my lord your son,
>> Prince Harry slain outright; and both the Blunts
>> Killed by the hand of Douglas.
>> Young Prince John and Westmoreland and Stafford
>>   fled the field;
>> And Harry Monmouth's brawn, the hulk Sir John,
>> Is prisoner to your son. O, such a day,
>> So fought, so followed, and so fairly won,
>> Came not till now to dignify the times
>> Since Caesar's fortunes!

> *Northumberland.*   How is this derived?
>> Saw you the field? Came you from Shrewsbury?

> *Lord Bardolph.*   I spake with one, my lord, that came
>> from thence,

70

A gentleman well bred and of good name,
That freely rendered me these news for true.

Enter Travers

Northumberland. Now, Travers, what good tidings
    comes with you?

Northumberland's associate, Travers, informs him of a gentleman who gave him "joyful tidings". But then a more authoritative horseman gave him the following message:

He told me that rebellion had bad luck
And that young Harry Percy's spur was cold.

Northumberland. Ha! Again.
    Said he young Harry Percy's spur was cold?
    Of Hotspur Coldspur? That rebellion
    Had met ill luck?

A third man, Morton, arrives. He comes from Shrewsbury with definitive news, including that of Hotspur's death.

Morton. The sum of all
    Is that the King hath won, and hath sent out
    A speedy power to encounter you, my lord,
    Under the conduct of young Lancaster [Prince John]
    And Westmoreland. This is the news at full.

Northumberland. Hence, therefore, thou nice crutch!
    A scaly gauntlet now with joints of steel
    Must glove this hand.

Morton tells of a further rebellion:

The gentle Archbishop of York is up

With well-appointed powers. He is a man
Who with a double surety binds his followers.
My lord your son had only but the corpse,
But shadows and the shows of men, to fight.

But now the Bishop
Turns insurrection to religion.
Supposed sincere and holy in his thoughts,
He's followed both with body and with mind,
And doth enlarge his rising with the blood
Of fair King Richard, scraped from Pomfret stones.

Richard was murdered at Pomfret Castle on Henry IV's order. Northumberland, after hearing all the news, prepares for war.

1.2   London: a street. Enter Sir John Falstaff, with his little Page bearing his sword and shield. Hal, as he indicated at Shrewsbury, has actually permitted Falstaff to carry off the honors of slaying Hotspur. The old rogue has been allotted a modest stipend and now is served by a page.

> *Falstaff.* Sirrah, you giant, what says the doctor
>   to my water?

> *Page.* He said, sir, the water itself was a good healthy
>   water; but for the party that owed it, he might
>   have more diseases than he knew for.

In other words, Falstaff has flunked a urinalysis. (He has, aptly enough, venereal disease.)

> *Falstaff.* Men of all sorts take a pride to gird at me.
>   The brain of this foolish compounded clay-man

is not able to invent anything on me. I am not
only witty in myself, but the cause that wit
is in other men.

He goes on to speak of Hal and their disreputable friend
Bardolph:

The Prince your master, whose chin is not yet
fledged – I will sooner have a beard grow in
the palm of my hand than he shall get one off
his cheek, and yet he will not stick to say his
face is a face-royal.

What said Master Dombledon about the satin for
my short cloak and my slops [full-cut breeches]?

Sporting his new reputation, Falstaff is disposed to deck
himself out.

Page. He said, sir, you should procure him better
assurance than Bardolph. He would not take his
band [bond] and yours. He liked not the security.

Falstaff. Let him be damned, like the glutton!
Pray God his tongue be hotter! A whoreson
Achitophel [a biblical traitor]! A rascally
yea-forsooth knave! To bear a gentleman in hand
and then stand upon security!

The Lord Chief Justice and his servant enter. The Justice
had sought Falstaff on the Gad's Hill caper, and had Prince
Henry arrested for striking him in court during a trial.
(Such apparently happened in history to the real Henry
before becoming Henry V.)

Page. Sir, here comes the nobleman that committed

the Prince for striking him about Bardolph.

Falstaff.   Wait close; I will not see him.

Chief Justice.   What's he that goes there?

Servant.   Falstaff, an't please your lordship.

Chief Justice.   He that was in question for the robbery?

Servant.   He, my lord. But he hath since done good service at Shrewsbury, and, as I hear, is now going with some charge to the Lord John of Lancaster.

Chief Justice.   What, to York! Call him back again.

Servant.   Sir John Falstaff.

Falstaff.   Boy, tell him I am deaf.

Page.   You must speak louder; my master is deaf.

Chief Justice.   I am sure he is, to the hearing of anything good. Go, pluck him by the elbow. I must speak with him.

Servant.   Sir John!

Falstaff.   What! a young knave, and begging! Is there not wars? Is there not employment?

Servant.   You mistake me, sir.

Falstaff.   Why, sir, did I say you were an honest man? setting my knighthood and my soldiership aside, I had lied in my throat if I had said so.

Chief Justice.   Sir John Falstaff, a word with you.

Falstaff.   My good lord! God give your lordship

good time of day. I am glad to see your lordship
abroad. I heard say your lordship was sick.
I hope your lordship goes abroad by advice.

Chief Justice. Sir John, I sent for you before your
expedition to Shrewsbury.

Falstaff. An't please your lordship, I hear his
Majesty is returned with some discomfort from
Wales.

Chief Justice. I talk not of his Majesty. You would
not come when I sent for you.

Falstaff. And I hear, moreover, his Highness is
fallen into this same whoreson apoplexy.

Chief Justice. Well, God mend him! I pray you, let
me speak with you. . . . I sent for you, when
there were matters against you for your life,
to come speak with me.

Falstaff. As I was then advised by my learned
counsel in the laws of this land-service, I did
not come.

Chief Justice. Well, the truth is, Sir John, you live in
great infamy. . . . Your means are very slender
and your waste is great.

Falstaff. I would it were otherwise. I would my
means were greater and my waist slenderer.

Chief Justice. You have misled the youthful Prince.

Falstaff. The young Prince hath misled me. I am
the fellow with the great belly, and he my dog.

Chief Justice. You follow the young Prince up and
down like his ill angel.

Falstaff. Not so, my lord. Your ill angel is light
[an "angel" was a coin; a bad one was depleted
of gold content, hence lighter], but I hope he that
looks upon me will take me without weighing.
You that are old consider not the capacities of
us that are young.

Chief Justice. Do you set down your name in the
scroll of youth, that are written down old with
all the characters of age? Have you not a moist
eye, a dry hand, a yellow cheek, a white beard,
a decreasing leg, and increasing belly? Is not
your voice broken, your wind short, your chin
double, your wit single, and every part about
you blasted with antiquity? And will you yet
call yourself young?

Falstaff. My lord, the truth is, I am only old in
judgment and understanding.

Chief Justice. God send the Prince a better companion.

Falstaff. God send the companion a better prince!
I cannot rid my hands of him.

Chief Justice. Well, the King hath severed you and
Prince Harry. I hear you are going with Lord
John of Lancaster against the Archbishop and the
Earl of Northumberland.

Falstaff. Yea, I thank your pretty sweet wit for it.
There is not a dangerous action can peep out his
head but I am thrust upon it. Well, I cannot last

76

ever. But it was always yet the trick of our
English nation, if they have a good thing, to
make it common.
  I wish to God my name were not so terrible
to the enemy as it is.

Chief Justice. Well, be honest, be honest, and God
  bless your expedition!

Falstaff. Will your lordship lend me a thousand
  pound to furnish me forth?

The Chief Justice has a summary answer for this:

  Not a penny, not a penny. Fare you well.
                    [exeunt Chief Justice and Servant

Falstaff. What money is in my purse?

Page. Seven groats and two pence.

Falstaff. I can get no remedy against this
  consumption of the purse. Borrowing only lingers
  and lingers it out, but the disease is incurable.

  Go bear this letter to my lord of Lancaster, this
  to the Prince, this to the Earl of Westmoreland,
  and this to old Mistress Ursula, whom I have
  weekly sworn to marry since I perceived the first
  white hair of my chin. About it. You know
  where to find me.

1.3 York: the Archbishop's palace. Enter the Archbishop,
Thomas Mowbray, and the lords Hastings and Bardolph.

  Archbishop. Thus have you heard our cause and

> known our means;
> And, my most noble friends, I pray you all,
> Speak plainly your opinions of our hopes.

They discuss matters, with particular reference to Northumberland.

> *Lord Bardolph.* The question, then, Lord Hastings, standeth thus:
> Whether our present five-and-twenty thousand
> May hold up head without Northumberland.

> *Hastings.* With him, we may.

> *Lord Bardolph.* Yea, marry, there's the point.
> But if without him we be thought too feeble,
> My judgment is, we should not step too far
> Till we had his assistance by the hand.

They recall the experience of Hotspur. And recall King Richard:

> *Archbishop.* They that, when Richard lived, would have him die,
> Are now enamoured on his grave.

> *Mowbray.* Shall we go draw our numbers and set on?

> *Hastings.* We are time's subjects, and time bids be gone.

Act II, scene 1. London: a street. Enter Mistress Quickly, hostess of the Boar's Head Tavern, officers Fang and Snare, and another.

> *Quickly.* Master Fang, have you entered the action [for debt]?

78

Fang. It is entered.

Quickly. Where's your yeoman? Is't a lusty yeoman?
will 'a [he] stand to't?

Fang (to Officer). Sirrah, where's Snare?

Snare. Here, here.

Fang. Snare, we must arrest Sir John Falstaff.

Snare. It may cost some of us our lives, for
he will stab.

Quickly. Alas the day! Take heed of him, he
stabbed me in mine own house, and that most
beastly. In good faith, 'a cares not what mischief
he does, if his weapon be out. He will foin like
any devil; he will spare neither man, woman, nor
child.

Mistress Quickly's use of "stabbed" and "weapon" has
more than one meaning. ("foin": to wield a weapon)

Fang. If I can close with him, I care not for his
thrust.

Quickly. No, nor I neither. I'll be at your elbow.
I am undone by his going. A hundred mark is a long
one for a poor lone woman to bear, and I have
borne and borne, and borne, and have been fubbed
off, and fubbed off, and fubbed off, from this day
to that day, that it is a shame to be thought on.
There is no honesty in such dealing.
    Yonder he comes, and that arrant malmsay-nose
knave, Bardolph, with him. Do your offices, do
your offices. Master Fang and Master Snare, do

me, do me, do me your offices.

Enter Falstaff, Page, and Bardolph

Falstaff. How now! Whose mare's dead? What's
the matter?

Fang. Sir John, I arrest you at the suit of
Mistress Quickly.

Falstaff. Away, varlets! Draw, Bardolph.
Cut me off the villain's head.

Quickly. Thou bastardly rogue!

Falstaff. Keep them off, Bardolph.

Quickly. Good people, bring a rescue or two.

Page. Away, you scullion! I'll tickle your
catastrophe [bottom, or perhaps some place else].

Enter Lord Chief Justice and his Men

Chief Justice. What is the matter? Keep the peace
here, ho!

Quickly. Good my lord, be good to me. I beseech
you, stand to me.

Chief Justice. How now, Sir John! What, are you
brawling here?

Quickly. O my most worshipful lord, an't please
your Grace, I am a poor widow of Eastcheap,
and he is arrested at my suit.

Chief Justice. For what sum?

Quickly. It is more than for some, my lord;
it is for all, all I have. He hath eaten me
out of house and home.

"Sum" and "some": Mistress Quickly is a rambling and word-mangling "character".

Chief Justice. How comes this, Sir John? Are you not
ashamed to enforce a poor widow to so rough a
course to come by her own?

Falstaff. What is the gross sum that I owe thee?

Quickly. Marry, if thou wert an honest man, thyself
and the money too. Thou didst swear to me upon a
parcel-gift goblet, sitting in my Dolphin-chamber,
at the round table, by a sea coal fire, upon
Wednesday in Wheeson week [Whitsun; Hostess
Quickly tends to take liberties with the English
language, although not perhaps to the extent that
Falstaff has taken liberties with her] when the
Prince broke thy head for liking his father to a
singing-man of Windsor, thou didst swear to me
then, as I was washing thy wound, to marry me
and make me my lady thy wife.

Falstaff. My lord, this is a poor mad soul, and she
says up and down the town that her eldest son is
like you.

Chief Justice. Sir John, I am well acquainted with your
manner of wrenching the true cause the false way.

[That was well said. He knows his man.]

You have, as it appears to me, practiced upon the

easy-yielding spirit of this woman, and made her serve your uses both in purse and in person.

Falstaff. I say to you, I do desire deliverance from these officers, being upon hasty employment in the King's affairs.

Chief Justice. Answer in the effect of your reputation, and satisfy the poor woman.

Falstaff. Come hither, hostess.

Falstaff does talk his way out of it, making more promises and obtaining another loan!

II.2 London: another street. Enter Prince Henry and Poins.

Prince. Before God, I am exceeding weary.

Poins. Is't come to that? I had thought weariness durst not have attached one of so high blood.

Prince. I tell thee, my heart bleeds inwardly that my father is so sick. And keeping such vile company as thou art hath in reason taken from me all ostentation [display] of sorrow.

Poins. The reason?

Prince. What wouldst thou think of me if I should weep?

Poins. I would think thee a most princely hypocrite.

Prince. And what accites your most worshipful thought to think so?

Poins. Why, because you have been so lewd and so
much engraffed to Falstaff.

Prince. And to thee.

Poins. By this light, I am well spoke on. I can hear
it with mine own ears.

Bardolph and the page of Falstaff arrive, Bardolph giving
Hal a letter from Falstaff. Poins reads it aloud:

"Sir John Falstaff, knight, to the son of the King,
nearest his father, Harry Prince of Wales, greeting."
Why this is a certificate [a legal instrument importing
the writer to be sovereign and the addressee subject].

Prince. Peace.

Poins (reads). "I commend me to thee, I commend thee,
and I leave thee. Be not too familiar with Poins,
for he misuses thy favors so much that he swears
thou art to marry his sister Nell. Repent at idle
times as thou mayest, and so farewell.
"Thine, by yea and no, which is as much as to
say, as thou usest him, Jack Falstaff with my
familiars, John with my brothers and sisters, and
Sir John with all Europe."
My lord, I'll steep this letter in sack and make
him eat it.

Prince (to Bardolph). Is your master here in London?

Bardolph. Yea, my lord.

Prince. Where sups he? Doth the old boar feed in the
old frank [sty]?

Bardolph. At the old place, my lord, in Eastcheap.

Prince. Sup any women with him?

Page. None, my lord, but old Mistress Quickly and
    Doll Tearsheet.

Prince. What pagan may that be?

Page. A proper gentlewoman, sir, and a kinswoman
    of my master's.

Prince. Even such kin as the parish heifers are
    to the town bull. [*to Poins*] Shall we steal upon
    them, Ned, at supper?

Poins. I am your shadow, my lord, I'll follow you.

II.3 Warkworth. Before the castle. Enter Northumberland,
his Wife, and the deceased Hotspur's wife, Lady Percy.
The women seek to talk him out of joining the rebellion.

Northumberland. Alas, sweet wife, my honor is at pawn,
    And, but my going, nothing can redeem it.

Lady Percy. O yet, for God's sake, go not to
        these wars!
    The time was, father, that you broke your word,
    When you were more endeared to it than now,
    When your own Percy, when my heart's dear Harry,
    Threw many a northward look to see his father
    Bring up his powers, but he did long in vain.
    Who then persuaded you to stay at home?

    O wondrous him!
    O miracle of men! – him did you leave,
    Second to none, unseconded by you,

84

To look upon the hideous god of war
In disadvantage.

Northumberland. Beshrew your heart,
Fair daughter, you do draw my spirits from me
With new lamenting ancient oversights.
But I must go and meet with danger there,
Or it will seek me in another place
And find me worse provided.

But his wife tells him, "Fly to Scotland," and the ever-shifty Northumberland will go there and await developments in England.

II.4   London.   The Boar's Head Tavern in Eastcheap.
Falstaff banters with Hostess Quickly and Doll Tearsheet.

Falstaff. If the cook help to make the gluttony,
you help to make the diseases, Doll. We catch
of you, Doll, we catch of you. Grant that, my
poor virtue, grant that.

A drawer [waiter] announces that Falstaff's crony Pistol has come into the tavern.

Doll. Hang him, swaggering rascal! Let him
not come hither. It is the foul-mouthed'st
rogue in England.

Enter Pistol, Bardolph, and Page

Pistol. God save you, Sir John!

Falstaff. Welcome, Ancient Pistol. Here,
Pistol, I charge you with a cup of sack.

Do you discharge upon mine hostess.

("Charge", "discharge", and "pistol" have second meanings.)

Pistol. I will discharge upon her, Sir John,
with two bullets.

Falstaff. She is pistol-proof, sir. You shall
hardly offend her.

Quickly. Come, I'll drink no proofs nor no bullets.
I'll drink no more than will do me good, for no
man's pleasure, I. ["bullets" also has another,
lewd meaning]

Pistol. Then to you, Mistress Dorothy; I will
charge you.

Doll. Charge me! I scorn you, scurvy companion.
What! you poor, base, rascally, cheating,
lack-linen mate! Away, you mouldy rogue, away!
I am meat for your master.

At Doll's behest, Falstaff, sword-in-hand, drives Pistol out
and is congratulated like a hero by Doll who promises to
"canvass thee between a pair of sheets" for his effort.

Enter music

Page. The music is come, sir.

Falstaff. Let them play. Play, sirs. Sit on my knee,
Doll. A rascal bragging slave! the rogue fled
from me like quicksilver.

Doll. I' faith, thou followedst him like a church
[perhaps, solid and unyielding]. Thou whoreson
little tidy Bartholomew boar-pig, when wilt thou

leave fighting o'days and foining o'nights, and
begin to patch up thine old body for heaven?

Enter, behind, Prince Henry and Poins,
disguised as waiters

Falstaff. Peace, good Doll! do not speak like a
death's-head. Do not bid me remember mine end.

Doll. Sirrah, what humor's the Prince of?

Falstaff. A good shallow young fellow. 'A [he]
would have made a good pantler [pantryman], 'a
would ha' chipped bread well.

Doll. They say Poins has a good wit.

Falstaff. He a good wit? Hang him, baboon! His wit's
as thick as Tewksbury mustard; there's no more
conceit [inventiveness] in him than is in a mallet.

Prince (alone to Poins, overhearing all Falstaff has said).
Would not this nave of a wheel have his ears
cut off?

Poins (alone to Hal). Let's beat him before his whore.

Prince (alone to Poins). Look, whether the withered
elder hath not his poll clawed like a parrot.

Poins (alone to Hal). Is it not strange that desire
should so many years outlive performance?

Falstaff. Thou dost give me flattering busses.

Falstaff calls for sack, Hal and Poins coming forward. As
they answer like waiters, "Anon, anon, sir," they simultaneously
reveal themselves.

Falstaff. Ha! a bastard son of the King's?
　　And art not thou Poins his brother?

Prince. Why, thou globe of sinful continents,
　　what a life dost thou lead!

Falstaff. Thou whoreson man compound of majesty,
　　by this light flesh and corrupt blood, thou art
　　welcome. ["flesh ... blood" referred to Doll]

Doll. How, you fat fool! I scorn you.

Prince. You whoreson candle-mine, you, how vilely
　　did you speak of me even now before this honest,
　　virtuous, civil gentlewoman!

Quickly. God's blessing of your good heart!

Falstaff. Didst thou hear me?

Prince. Yea, and you knew me, as you did when you
　　ran away by Gad's Hill. You knew I was at your
　　back, and spoke it on purpose to try my patience.

Falstaff. No, no, no; not so. I did not think thou
　　wast within hearing.

Prince. I shall drive you then to confess the
　　wilful abuse, and then I know how to handle you.

Falstaff. No abuse, Hal, o' mine honor, no abuse.

Prince. Not to dispraise me, and call me pantler
　　and bread-chipper and I know not what?

Poins. No abuse?

Falstaff. No abuse, Ned, i' the world; honest Ned,
　　none. I dispraised him before the wicked, that

the wicked might not fall in love with him; in
which doing, I have done the part of a careful
friend and a true subject, and thy father is to
give me thanks for it. [The artful dodger is at
his accustomed work.]

Prince. See now, whether pure fear and entire
cowardice doth not make thee wrong this virtuous
gentlewoman to close with us [appease us]. Is
she of the wicked? or is the boy of the wicked? or
honest Bardolph, whose zeal burns in his nose,
of the wicked?

Poins. Answer, thou dead elm, answer.

Falstaff. The fiend hath pricked down Bardolph,
irrecoverable, and his face is Lucifer's
privy-kitchen, where he doth nothing but roast
maltworms [habitual drinkers]. For the boy
there is a good angel about him, but the devil
outbids him too.

Prince. For the women?

Falstaff. For one of them, she is in hell already, and
burns poor souls. For the other, I owe her money,
and whether she be damned for that, I know not.

Knocking within

Quickly. Who knocks so loud at door?
Look to the door there, Francis.

Enter Peto

Peto tells the Prince that his father is preparing for war,
and that there are "a dozen captains, bare-headed, sweating,

knocking at the taverns, and asking every one for Sir John Falstaff".

> *Prince.* By heaven, Poins, I feel me much to blame,
> So idly to profane the precious time,
> When tempest of commotion, like the south
> Borne with black vapor, doth begin to melt
> And drop upon our bare unarmed heads.
>
> Give me my sword and cloak. Falstaff, goodnight.

Hal is serious, if nothing else because he spoke that last passage in poetry, unlike the previous fun in prose.

Prince Henry, Poins, Peto and Bardolph depart, leaving Falstaff to express a certain regret:

> Now comes in the sweetest morsel of the night,
> and we must hence and leave it [i.e. her] unpicked.

> *Knocking, and re-enter Bardolph*

Falstaff. How now! What's the matter?

Bardolph. You must away to Court, sir,
> presently. A dozen captains stay at door for you.

Falstaff (*to the Page*). Pay the musicians, sirrah.
> Farewell, hostess. Farewell, Doll. You see, my
> good wenches, how men of merit are sought after.
> The undeserver may sleep, when the man of action
> is called on. Farewell, good wenches.

Doll. I cannot speak. If my heart be not ready to
> burst -- well, sweet Jack, have a care of thyself.

Falstaff departs for the war, Doll and Hostess Quickly blubbering in his wake.

Act III, scene 1. Westminster. The Palace. The King enters in his nightgown, with a Page. The latter receives instructions, and exits.

King. How many thousands of my poorest subjects
    Are at this hour asleep! O Sleep, O gentle Sleep,
    Nature's soft nurse, how have I frighted thee
    That thou no more wilt weigh my eyelids down
    And steep my senses in forgetfulness?

    O thou dull god, why liest thou with the vile
    In loathsome beds, and leavest the kingly couch
    A watch-case or a common 'larum bell?
    Uneasy lies the head that wears a crown.

Enter the earls of Warwick and Surrey

King. They say the Bishop and Northumberland
    Are fifty thousand strong.

Warwick. It cannot be, my lord.
    Rumor doth double, like the voice and echo,
    The numbers of the feared. Please it your Grace
    To go to bed. Upon my soul, my lord,
    The powers that you already have sent forth
    Shall bring this prize in very easily.

    To comfort you the more, I have received
    A certain instance that Glendower is dead.
    Your Majesty hath been this fortnight ill,
    And these unseasoned hours perforce must
    Add unto your sickness.

King. I will take your counsel.
    And were these inward wars once out of hand,

> We would, dear lords, unto the Holy Land.
>
> [*exeunt*

This is thematic with Henry IV: King Richard's blood is on his hand, his deceitful ways have also alienated former allies into rebellion, he cannot sleep as a result, and assuages his troubled conscience with thoughts of eventually going to Palestine.

III.2   Gloucestershire.   Before Justice Shallow's house. Enter Shallow and Silence meeting, both country justices; and Mouldy, Shadow, Wart, Feeble, Bullcalf (who appear in all their woebegoneness on the cover of our book).

> *Shallow.* Come on, come on, come on, sir. Give me
> your hand, sir, give me your hand, sir. An early
> stirrer, by the rood! And how doth my good
> cousin Silence?
>
> *Silence.* Good morrow, good cousin Shallow.

They chat about 'the good old days'. Among Shallow's old pals and acquaintances he mentions someone familiar to us also:

> Then was Jack Falstaff, now Sir John, a boy,
> and page to Thomas Mowbray, Duke of Norfolk.
>
> *Silence.* This Sir John, cousin, that comes hither
> anon about soldiers?
>
> *Shallow.* The same Sir John, the very same.
> I see him break Skogan's head at the court-gate,
> when 'a was a crack not thus high. And the very
> same day did I fight with one Sampson Stockfish,

a fruiter, behind Gray's Inn. Jesu, Jesu, the mad
days that I have spent! and to see how many of my
old acquaintances are dead!

Silence. We shall all follow, cousin.

Shallow. Certain, 'tis certain; very sure, very sure.

Shallow is a rather eccentric character, not far short of being
a true 'fantastick'.

Enter Bardolph and one with him

Bardolph. Good morrow, honest gentlemen.
I beseech you, which is Justice Shallow?

Shallow. I am Robert Shallow, sir; a poor esquire
of this county, and one of the King's justices of
the peace. What is your good pleasure with me?

Bardolph. My captain, sir, commends him to you;
my captain, Sir John Falstaff, a tall gentleman
[tall: brave], by heaven, and a most gallant leader.

Speaking of the devil, the gallant walks in. He comes with
the legal authority to impress poor souls into military service.

Falstaff. Fie! this is hot weather, gentlemen.
Have you provided me here half a dozen sufficient
men?

Shallow. Marry, have we sir. Will you sit?

Falstaff. Let me see them, I beseech you.

Shallow. Where's the roll? Where's the roll?
Where's the roll? Let me see. Let me see.
Let me see. So, so, so, so, so, so, so. Yea,
marry, sir. Ralph Mouldy! Let them appear as

I call. Let me see. Where is Ralph Mouldy?

Mouldy. Here, an't please you.

Falstaff. Is thy name Mouldy?

Mouldy. Yea, an't please you.

Falstaff. 'Tis the more time thou wert used.

Shallow. Ha, ha, ha! most excellent, i' faith! things that are mouldy lack use; very singular good!

Falstaff. Prick him. [Mark him down.]

Mouldy. I was pricked well enough before ["prick" has a second meaning], an you could have let me alone. My old dame will be undone now for one to do her husbandry and her drudgery. You need not to have pricked me; there are other men fitter to go out than I.

It avails him nothing. Mouldy finds himself pricked again.

Shallow. Let me see. Simon Shadow!

Falstaff. Yea, marry, let me have him to sit under. He's like to be a cold soldier.

Shallow. Where's Shadow?

Shadow. Here, Sir.

Falstaff. Shadow, whose son art thou?

Shadow. My mother's son, sir.

Shallow. Do you like him, Sir John?

Falstaff. Shadow will serve for summer.

Prick him.

Shallow. Thomas Wart!

Wart. Here, sir.

Falstaff. Thou art a very ragged wart. [See the cover
and you will spot him.]

Shallow. Shall I prick him down, Sir John?

Falstaff. It were superfluous, for his apparel is built
upon his back and the whole frame stands upon
pins. Prick him no more.

Shallow. Francis Feeble!

Feeble. Here, sir.

Falstaff. What trade art thou, Feeble?

Feeble. A woman's tailor, sir.

A little more ribaldry (a tailor pricks with his pin), and
Feeble escapes not unpricked. The same for Bullcalf, in
spite of his whoreson cough and cold.

Falstaff and the two Justices go to dinner, Bullcalf then
easing up to Bardolph:

> Good Master Corporate Bardolph, stand
> my friend, and here's four Harry ten shillings
> in French crowns for you. In very truth, sir,
> I had as lief be hanged, sir, as go. And yet, for
> mine own part, sir, I do not care. But rather,
> because I am unwilling, and, for mine own part,
> have a desire to stay with my friends; else, sir,
> I did not care, for mine own part, so much.

Bardolph. Go to, stand aside.

Mouldy does the same, and may also "stand aside". Falstaff and the Justices re-enter.

Falstaff. Come, sir, which men shall I have?

Shallow. Four of which you please.

Bardolph (aside to Falstaff). Sir, a word with you. I have three pound to free Mouldy and Bullcalf.

Shallow. Come, Sir John, which four will you have?

Falstaff. Do you choose for me.

Shallow. Marry, then, Mouldy, Bullcalf, Feeble and Shadow.

Falstaff. Mouldy and Bullcalf; for you, Mouldy, stay at home till you are past service. And for your part, Bullcalf, grow till you come unto it. I will none of you.

Shallow. Sir John, Sir John, do not yourself wrong. They are your likeliest men, and I would have you served with the best.

Falstaff. Will you tell me, Master Shallow, how to choose a man? Care I for the limb, the thews, the stature, bulk, and big assemblance of a man! Give me the **spirit**, Master Shallow.

Falstaff goes on to praise Wart, Shadow, and Feeble, Shadow especially for being so thin the enemy cannot take aim at him. "O give me," he says, "the spare men, and spare me the great ones."

Falstaff. These fellows will do well, Master Shallow. God keep you, Master Silence. I will not use many

words with you. Fare you well, gentlemen both. I
thank you. I must a dozen mile tonight. Bardolph,
give the soldiers coats.

Shallow. Sir John, the Lord bless you! God prosper
your affairs! At your return visit our house. Let
our old acquaintance be renewed. Peradventure
I will with ye to the Court.

Falstaff. 'Fore God, I would you would, Master
Shallow. Fare you well, gentle gentlemen.

When Falstaff is alone, he has a few words to say about
Shallow's rendition of his own exuberant feats back in the
'good old days':

Lord, lord, how subject we old men are to this
vice of lying! This same starved justice hath
done nothing but prate to me of the wildness of
his youth, and the feats he hath done about
Turnbull Street; and every third word a lie.

Yet Falstaff sees that Shallow has some money and thinks
Falstaff has influence at Court. The scoundrel promises to
return to Gloucestershire.

Act IV, scene 1. Yorkshire: Gaultree Forest. Enter the
Archbishop of York, Mowbray, Hastings, and others, the
enemy army at no great distance from theirs.

Archbishop. My friends and brethren in these great
affairs,
I must acquaint you that I have received
New-dated letters from Northumberland,

Their cold intent, tenor, and substance, thus:
Here doth he wish his person, with such powers
As might hold sortance with his quality,
The which he could not levy. Whereupon
He is retired, to ripe his growing fortunes,
To Scotland. And concludes in hearty prayers
That your attempts may outlive the hazard
And fearful meeting of their opposite.

Mowbray. Thus do the hopes we have in him
        touch ground
    And dash themselves to pieces.

The Archbishop used the term "**cold** intent". Shakespeare echoed the Hotspur-"**Cold**spur" reference by Northumberland in the First Act to remind us that the previously "crafty-sick" Northumberland has once again abandoned those who relied upon him.

Enter a Messenger

Hastings. Now, what news?

Messenger. West of this forest, scarcely off a mile,
    In goodly form comes on the enemy.
    And, by the ground they hide, I judge their number
    Upon or near the rate of thirty thousand.

Mowbray. The just proportion that we gave them out.
    Let us sway on and face them in the field.

The numbers on each side are fairly even, and Mowbray is keen to fight. His father and Bolingbroke (now Henry IV) were adversaries who were stopped by King Richard II from waging a trial by combat. The elder Mowbray was banished and died in exile. (See Shakespeare's *Richard II*.)

Archbishop. What well-appointed leader fronts
    us here?

Enter Westmoreland

Mowbray. I think it is my lord of Westmoreland.

Westmoreland. Health and fair greeting from our
    general,
    The Prince, Lord John and Duke of Lancaster.

Archbishop. Say on my Lord of Westmoreland,
    in peace.
    What doth concern your coming?

Westmoreland. Wherefore do you so ill translate
    yourself
    Out of the speech of peace that bears such grace,
    Into the harsh and boisterous tongue of war,
    Turning your books to graves, your ink to blood,
    Your pens to lances and your tongue divine
    To a loud trumpet and a point of war?

Archbishop. Wherefore do I this?
    Briefly to this end: We are all diseased,
    . . . of which disease
    Our late king, Richard, being infected, died.

Henry IV is of course that "disease", Bolingbroke having
usurped Richard's throne and then instigated his death.

    When we are wronged and would unfold our griefs,
    We are denied access unto his [the King's] person.

Westmoreland denies any wrongs having been committed
and that the King ever denied the Archbishop an audience.
Mowbray speaks of his father:

The King [Richard] that loved him as the state
   stood then,
Was force perforce compelled to banish him.
And then that Henry Bolingbroke and he,
Being mounted and both roused in their seats,
Their neighing coursers daring of the spur,
Their armed staves in charge, their beavers
   [helmets] down,
Their eyes of fire sparkling through sights of
   steel
And the loud trumpet blowing them together,
Then, then, when there was nothing could have
   stayed
My father from the breast of Bolingbroke,
O, when the King did throw his warder down
   [to stop the fight],
His own life hung upon the staff he threw.
Then threw he down himself and all their lives
That by indictment and by dint of sword
Have since miscarried under Bolingbroke.

Westmoreland. You speak, Lord Mowbray,
   now you know not what.
Here come I from our princely general
To know your griefs; to tell you from his Grace
That he will give you audience; and wherein
It shall appear that your demands are just,
You shall enjoy them, everything set off
   [discounted]
That might so much as think you enemies.

Mowbray. But he hath forced us to compel this offer,
And it proceeds from policy, not love.

100

Westmoreland. Mowbray, you overween to take it so.
 This offer comes from mercy, not from fear.

Mowbray. Well, by my will we shall admit no parley.

Westmoreland. That argues but the shame of your
  offence.
 A rotten case abides no handling.

Hastings. Hath the Prince John a full commission,
 In very ample virtue of his father,
 To bear and absolutely to determine
 Of what conditions we shall stand upon?

Westmoreland. That is intended in the general's name.
 I muse you make so slight a question.

Archbishop. Then take, my Lord of Westmoreland,
  this schedule,
 For this contains our general grievances.

Westmoreland. This will I show the general.
 Please you, lords,
 In sight of both our battles we may meet,
 And either end in peace, which God so frame!
 Or to the place of differences call the swords
 Which must decide it.
                              [*exit Westmoreland*

Mowbray is suspicious and useasy:

 There is a thing within my bosom tells me
 That no conditions of our peace can stand.

Hastings. Fear you not that. If we can make
  our peace,
 Upon such large terms and so absolute

> As our conditions shall consist upon,
> Our peace shall stand as firm as rocky mountains.

Mowbray. Yea, but our valuation shall be such
> That every slight and false-derived cause,
> Yea, every idle, nice, and wanton reason
> Shall to the King taste of this action.

Archbishop. No, no, my lord. Note this:
> the King is weary
> Of dainty and such picking grievances [trifles].
> For he hath found to end one doubt by death
> Revives two greater in the heirs of life.

He believes the King realizes that assailing them by breaking any agreement they make would incite others to rebel, so the King must understand the folly of not keeping his word. Hastings seconds the Archbishop, maintaining that the King simply lacks the power to harm them. Mowbray can only acquiesce. At that point, Westmoreland returns with news that Prince John will meet them in a place between their mutual armies.

IV.2 Another part of the forest. The archbishop, Mowbray, Hastings and others come from one side; Prince John of Lancaster, Westmoreland and others come from the opposite side.

Prince John. You are well encountered here,
> my cousin Mowbray.
> Good day to you, gentle Lord Archbishop.
> And so to you, Lord Hastings, and to all.

Archbishop. I sent your Grace

The parcels and particulars of our grief,
Whereon this Hydra son of war is born,
  [Hydra: the serpent of many heads,
  slain by Hercules]
Whose dangerous eyes may well be charmed asleep
With grant of our most just and right desires,
And true obedience, of this madness cured,
Stoop tamely to the foot of majesty.

Mowbray. If not, we ready are to try our fortunes
To the last man.

Westmoreland. Pleaseth your Grace to answer them
    directly
How far forth you do like their articles.

Prince John. I like them all, and do allow them well,
And swear here, by the honor of my blood,
My father's purposes have been mistook.
My lord, these griefs shall be with speed redressed.
Upon my soul, they shall.

If this may please you,
Discharge your powers unto their several counties,
As we will ours. And here between the armies
Let's drink together friendly and embrace,
That all their eyes may bear those tokens home
Of our restored love and amity.

Archbishop. I take your princely word for these
    redressed.

Prince John. I give it to you, and will maintain
    my word.
And thereupon I drink unto your Grace.

Hastings. Go, captain, and deliver to the army
This news of peace. Let them have pay, and part.
I know it will well please them. Hie thee, captain.
[*exit Officer*

Archbishop (*toasting*). To you, my noble Lord of
Westmoreland.

Westmoreland. I pledge your Grace. My love to ye
Shall show itself more openly hereafter.

Archbishop. I do not doubt you.

Westmoreland. I am glad of it.
Health to my lord and gentle cousin, Mowbray.

Mowbray. You wish me health in very happy season,
For I am, on the sudden, something ill.

Archbishop. Believe me, I am passing light in spirit.

Mowbray. So much the worse, if your own rule be true.

Shouts can be heard.

Prince John. The word of peace is rendered.
Hark, how they shout!

Mowbray. This had been cheerful after victory.

Archbishop. A peace is of the nature of a conquest,
For then both parties nobly are subdued,
And neither party loser.

Prince John (*to Westmoreland*). Go, my lord,
And let me our army be discharged too.
[*exit Westmoreland*
And, good my lord, so please you, let our trains
March by us, that we may peruse the men

104

We should have coped withal.

Archbishop. Go, good Lord Hastings,
And ere they be dismissed, let them march by.

[exit Hastings

Prince John. I trust, lords, we shall lie
Tonight together.

Westmoreland returns and Prince John asks him,

Now cousin, wherefore stands our army still?

Westmoreland. The leaders, having charge from you
to stand,
Will not go off until they hear you speak.

Prince John. They know their duties.

Hastings returns, and announces:

My lord, our army is dispersed already.
Like youthful steers unyoked, they take their
courses
East, west, north, south; or, like a school broke up,
Each hurries toward his home and sporting-place.

Westmoreland. Good tidings, my Lord Hastings,
for the which
I do arrest thee, traitor, of high treason.
And you, Lord Archbishop, and you, Lord
Mowbray,
Of capital treason I attach you both.

Mowbray. Is this proceeding just and honorable?

Westmoreland. Is your assembly so?

Archbishop. Will you thus break your faith?

Prince John. I pawned thee none.
   I promised you redress of these same grievances
   Whereof you did complain; which, by mine honor,
   I will perform with a most Christian care.
   But you, rebels, look to taste the due
   Meet for rebellion and such acts as yours.

   Some guard these traitors to the block of death,
   Treason's true bed and yielder up of breath.

A true son of Bolingbroke is Prince John.

IV.3   Another part of the forest.   Alarum.   Enter Falstaff, arriving late to battle, running into Coleville, one of the enemy.

Falstaff. What's your name, sir? of what
   condition are you, and of what place, I pray?

Coleville. I am a knight, sir, and my name is
   Coleville of the Dale.

Falstaff. Well, then, Coleville is your name,
   a knight is your degree, and your place the
   Dale. Coleville shall be still your name, a
   traitor your degree, and the dungeon your
   place, a place deep enough. So shall you be
   still Coleville of the dale. [dale: valley, so
   a dungeon is low like a valley]

Coleville. Are you not Sir John Falstaff?

Falstaff. As good a man as he, sir, whoe'er
   I am. Do ye yield, sir? or shall I sweat for you?
   If I do sweat, they are the drops of thy lovers,

106

and they weep for thy death.
Therefore, rouse up fear and trembling, and do
observance to my mercy.

Coleville. I think you are Sir John Falstaff, and
in that thought yield me.

(This is an example of Shakespeare's echoing humor, if one
recalls Falstaff's empty bragging to the Chief Justice in the
First Act: "I would to God my name were not so terrible to
the enemy as it is." His malodorous stabbing of Hotspur's
corpse has gained him not only currency but rather
widespread repute!)

Unparenthetically, I am obliged to add that, as previously
mentioned and contrary to much opinion, Falstaff is not a
true-bred coward. He is not a coward at all, unless we may
cite him a coward on policy, a most judicious coward, but
not a devout, religious one. He arrives tardy to battle
because that appears only sensible to one who scorns
"Honor". Yet once arrived, and meeting an armed and
probably dangerous adversary (but not so dangerous
certainly as a Douglas or, Heaven forfend, a Hotspur), he
not only stands his ground but displays a marvellous
confidence. That this "brawn" and "bulk" is uplifted by his
impudently-won reputation may account for some of the
bravado, sauciness, but by no means all. There's nobody
backing him here. In such a situation, a true-bred coward
would have 'come to his senses'.

Enter Prince John of Lancaster

Prince John. Now, Falstaff, where have you been
all this while?
Falstaff. I never knew yet but rebuke and check

was the reward of valor. I have speeded hither
with the very extremest inch of possibility.
I have foundered nine score and odd posts, and
here, travel-tainted as I am, have, in my pure
and immaculate valor, taken Sir John Coleville
of the Dale, a most furious knight and valorous
enemy.
But what of that? He saw me, and yielded, that
I may justly say, with the hook-nosed fellow of
Rome, "I came, I saw, and overcame."

As exasperating as Falstaff's association with Julius Caesar
may seem, it did rather happen that way.

Prince John. It was more of his courtesy than
your deserving.

Falstaff. I know not. Here he is, and here
I yield him. And I beseech your Grace, let
it be booked with the rest of this day's deeds, or,
by the Lord, I will have it in a particular ballad
else, with mine own picture on the top on't,
Coleville kissing my foot.

Westmoreland enters, John instructing him to take Coleville
and others to York for execution. He himself will proceed
to Westminster where his father the King "is sore sick".

Falstaff. My lord, I beseech you, give me leave to go
Through Gloucestershire, and, when you come
to Court,
Stand my good lord, pray, in your good report.

Prince John. Fare you well, Falstaff. I, in my condition
Shall better speak of you than you deserve.

108

Alone, Falstaff speaks in soliloquy frankly of princes and famously of sack wine:

> Good faith, this same young sober-blooded boy
> doth not love me. Nor a man cannot make him
> laugh; but that's no marvel, he drinks no wine.

> A good sherris-sack hath a two-fold operation
> in it. It ascends me into the brain, dries me there
> all the foolish and dull and crudy vapors which
> environ it; makes it apprehensive, quick, forgetive,
> full of nimble, fiery, and delectable shapes, which,
> delivered o'er to the voice, the tongue, which is
> the birth, becomes excellent wit.

> The second property of your excellent sherris is
> the warming of the blood, which, before cold and
> settled, left the liver white and pale, which is the
> badge of pusillanimity and cowardice. But the
> sherris warms it and makes it course from the
> inwards to the parts extreme.

> Herein comes it that Prince Henry is valiant, for
> the cold blood he did naturally inherit of his father,
> he hath, like lean, sterile, and bare land, manured,
> husbanded, and tilled with excellent endeavor of
> drinking good and good store of fertile sherris,
> that he is become very hot and valiant.

> If I had a thousand sons, the first humane principle
> I would teach them would be to forswear thin
> potation and to addict themselves to sack.

Bardolph enters, informing Falstaff that the army has been discharged.

Falstaff. Let them go. I'll through Gloucestershire
    and there will I visit Master Robert Shallow,
    esquire. I have him already tempering between
    my finger and thumb, and shortly will I seal
    with him. Come away.

Falstaff, after taking his advantage of Mistress Quickly, and
pocketing recruitment 'gratuities', now seeks an ill-advised
'loan' from the suitably-impressed Master Shallow.

IV.4   Westminster: the Jerusalem Chamber. The ill King
Henry expresses to his sons Thomas of Clarence and
Humphrey of Gloucester his fears for the future of the realm
when he dies and Prince Henry occupies the throne.

King. My grief stretches itself beyond the hour
    of death.
    The blood weeps from my heart when I do shape
    In forms imaginary the unguided days
    And rotten times that you shall look upon
    When I am sleeping with my ancestors.
    For when his headstrong riot hath no curb,
    When rage and hot blood are his counsellors,
    When means and lavish manners meet together,
    O, with what wings shall his affections fly
    Towards fronting peril and opposed decay!

However, the King had something positive to say about
Hal's temperament, which perhaps manifests his liking for
the Prince and undying hope that he has mettle in him:

    He is gracious, if he be observed.
    He hath a tear for pity and a hand

Open as day for melting charity.
Yet notwithstanding, being incensed, he's flint,
As humorous as winter and as sudden
As flaws congealed in the spring of day.
His temper, therefore, must be well observed.

Westmoreland enters with joyful tidings: the defeat of the
Archbishop, and following this comes the announcement
that an army led by Northumberland has been overthrown
(finally he fights, but waited too long). Welcome news, but
the King's illness worsens and his thoughts are on his health
and on the impending, worrisome reign of Prince Henry.

> *King.* Wherefore should these good news make
> me sick?
> I pray you, take me up, and bear me hence
> Into some other chamber. Softly, pray.

IV.5 Another chamber. The King asks those in attendance,

> Set me the crown upon my pillow here.

> *Clarence* (*to the others*). His eye is hollow,
> and he changes much.

> *Warwick.* Less noise, less noise!

Prince Henry now makes his appearance in the chamber.

> *Warwick.* Not so much noise, my lords.
> Sweet prince, speak low.
> The King your father is disposed to sleep.

> *Clarence.* Let us withdraw into the other room.

> *Warwick.* Will't please your Grace to go along with us?

Prince Henry. No, I will sit and watch here
    by the King.
                       [*exeunt all but the Prince*
    Why doth the crown lie there upon his pillow,
    Being so troublesome a bedfellow?
    O polished perturbation! Golden care!

Hal believes his father has died:

    My gracious lord! My father!
    This sleep is sound indeed; this is a sleep
    That from this golden rigol hath divorced
    So many English kings. Thy due from me
    Is tears and heavy sorrows of the blood,
    Which nature, love, and fillial tenderness
    Shall, O dear father, pay thee plenteously.
    My due from thee is this imperial crown,
    Which, as immediate from thy place and blood,
    Derives itself to me.

Hal puts on the crown, and leaves the room.

King (awakening). Warwick! Gloucester! Clarence!

They come in and tell him that Prince Henry had been with him.

King. Where is the crown? Who took it from my
    pillow?

Warwick. When we withdrew, my liege, we left it here.

King. The Prince hath ta'en it hence.
    Go, seek him out.
    Is he so hasty that he doth suppose
    My sleep my death?

Find him, my Lord of Warwick. Chide him hither.

Hal re-enters, and the King tells the others to leave them
alone together. They depart.

Prince. I never thought to hear you speak again.

King. Thy wish was father, Harry, to that thought.
I stay too long by thee, I weary thee.
Dost thou so hunger for mine empty chair
That thou wilt needs invest thee with my
  honors
Before thy hour be ripe? O foolish youth!
Thou hast stolen that which after some few
  hours
Were thine without offense.

Thy life did manifest thou lovedst me not,
And thou wilt have me die assured of it.
Thou hidst a thousand daggers in thy thoughts,
Which thou whetted on thy stony heart
To stab at half an hour of my life.

The King discloses to the Prince the great fears he has for
the security of the realm once Hal has charge:

Pluck down my officers, break my decrees,
For now a time is come to mock at form.
Harry the Fifth is crowned. Up, vanity!
Down, royal state! All you sage counsellors,
  hence!
And to the English court assemble now,
From every region, apes of idleness!

Now, neighbor confines, purge you of your scum.
Have you a ruffian that will swear, drink, dance,

113

Revel the night, rob, murder, and commit
The oldest sins the newest kind of ways?
Be happy, he will trouble you no more.
England shall give him office, honor, might,
For the Fifth Harry from curbed license plucks
The muzzle of restraint, and the wild dog
Shall flesh his tooth on every innocent.

O my poor kingdom, sick with civil blows!
When that my care could not withhold thy riots,
What wilt thou do when riots is thy care?
O, thou wilt be a wilderness again,
Peopled with wolves, thy old inhabitants!

The Prince replies.

God witness with me, when I here came in,
And found no course of breath within your
    Majesty,
How cold it struck my heart! If I do feign,
O, let me in my present wildness die
And never live to show the incredulous world
The noble change that I have purposed!

Coming to look on you, thinking you dead,
And dead almost [myself] to think you were,
I spake unto this crown as having sense,
And thus upbraided it: "The care on thee
    depending
Hath fed upon the body of my father.
Therefore, thou best of gold art worst of gold.
Thou, most fine, most honored, most renowned,
Hast eat thy bearer up." Thus, my most royal
    liege,

Accusing it, I put it on my head,
To try with it, as with an enemy.

But if it did infect my blood with joy,
Or swell my thoughts to any strain of pride,
Let God for ever keep it from my head
And make me as the poorest vassal is
That doth with awe and terror kneel to it!

King. O my son,
     God put it in thy mind to take it hence,
     That thou mightest win the more thy father's
       love,
     Pleading so wisely in excuse of it.

     Come hither, Harry, sit thou by my bed,
     And hear, I think, the very latest counsel
     That ever I shall breathe.

     God knows, my son,
     By what bypaths and indirekt crooked ways
     I met this crown. And I myself know well
     How troublesome it sat upon my head.
     To thee it shall descend with better quiet,
     Better opinion, better confirmation,
     For all the soil of the achievement goes
     With me into the earth.

     Yet, though thou stand'st more sure than
      I could do,
     Thou art not firm enough, since griefs are green,
     And all my friends, which thou must make thy
      friends,
     Have but their stings and teeth newly ta'en out,
     By whose fell working I was first advanced

> And by whose power I well might lodge a fear
> To be again displaced, which to avoid,
> I cut them off.

His allies raised him up, from which position he cut them down. The King tells the Prince he had planned "to lead out many to the Holy Land, to keep them away from his throne".

> Therefore, my Harry,
> Be it thy course to busy giddy minds
> With foreign quarrels.

Thus the policy behind some foreign policy.

> How I came by the crown, O God forgive,
> And grant it may with thee in true peace live.

Prince John arrives. Warwick and others likewise enter the room.

> *King.* Doth any name particular belong
> Unto the lodging where I first did swoon?

> *Warwick.* 'Tis called Jerusalem, my noble lord.

> *King.* Laud be to God! Even there my life must end.
> It hath been prophesied to me many years,
> I should not die but in Jerusalem,
> Which vainly I supposed the Holy Land.
> But bear me to that chamber. There I'll lie.

Always the opportunist is the Bolingbroke King.

Act V, scene 1. Gloucestershire: Shallow's house. Enter Shallow, Falstaff, Bardolph, and Page.

Shallow. By cock and pie, sir, you shall not away
    tonight. What, Davy, I say!

Falstaff. You must excuse me, Master Robert
    Shallow.

Shallow. I will not excuse you; you shall not be
    excused; excuses shall not be admitted; there is
    no excuse shall serve; you shall not be excused.
    Why, Davy!

Enter Davy

Shallow. Some pigeons, Davy, a couple of
    short-legged hens, a joint of mutton, and
    any pretty little tiny kickshaws [dainties],
    tell William cook.

Davy. Doth the man of war stay all night, sir?

Shallow. Yea, Davy. I will use him well.
    A friend i'Court is better than a penny in purse.
    Use his men well, Davy, for they are arrant knaves
    and will backbite.

Davy. No worse than they are backbitten, sir, for
    they have marvellous foul linen.

Shallow. Well conceited, Davy. About thy business,
    Davy.

Davy. I beseech, you, sir, to countenance [support]
    William Visor of Woncot against Clement Perkes
    of the hill.

(Shallow, of course, is a justice of the peace, and his man
Davy wants the justice to favor his friend in a lawsuit.)

Shallow. There is many complaints, Davy, against
that Visor. That Visor is an arrant knave, on
my knowledge.

Davy. I grant your worship that he is a knave, sir,
but yet, God forbid, sir, but a knave should have
some countenance at his friend's request. An honest
man, sir, is able to speak for himself, when a knave
is not. I have served your worship truly, sir, this
eight years, and if I cannot once or twice in a
quarter bear out a knave against an honest man, I
have but a very little credit with your worship.
The knave is mine honest friend, sir. Therefore,
I beseech your worship, let him be countenanced.

Shallow. Go to [Enough], I say he shall have no
wrong. Look about, Davy.   [exit Davy, his
out-and-out knave of a friend Visor evidently
countenanced]

Shallow now turns to Falstaff:

Where are you, Sir John? Come, come, come,
off with your boots. Give me your hand,
Master Bardolph.

When Falstaff is alone, he has this to say about the eccentric
(Falstaff thinks, foolish) Justice Shallow:

I will devise matter enough out of this Shallow
to keep Prince Henry in continual laughter the
wearing out of six fashions.

V.2   Westminster: the Palace. Warwick and the Lord Chief
Justice meet.

Chief Justice. How doth the King?

Warwick. Exceeding well. His cares are now
all ended.

Chief Justice. I hope, not dead.

Warwick. He's walked the way of nature,
And to our purposes he lives no more.

Chief Justice. I would his Majesty had called me
with him.
The service that I truly did his life
Hath left me open to all injuries.

Warwick. Indeed I think the young King loves
you not.

Chief Justice. I know he doth not.

*Enter the new King's brothers John, Thomas (of Clarence),
and Humphrey (Gloucester), Westmoreland and others*

Chief Justice. O God, I fear all will be overturned!

Clarence. Well, you must now speak Sir John
Falstaff fair,
Which swims against your stream of quality.

Chief Justice. If truth and upright innocency fail me,
I'll to the King my master that is dead,
And tell him who hath sent me after him.

Enter King Henry the Fifth, attended

Chief Justice. Good morrow, and God save Your

Majesty!

King. This new and gorgeous garment, majesty,
Sits not so easy on me as you think.
Brothers, you mix your sadness with some fear.
This is the English, not the Turkish court.
You all look strangely on me, and [*to the
Chief Justice*] you most.
You are, I think, assured I love you not.

Chief Justice. I am assured, if I be measured rightly,
Your Majesty hath no just cause to hate me.

King. No?
How might a prince of my great hopes forget
So great indignities you laid upon me?
What! rate, rebuke, and roughly send to prison
The immediate heir of England! Was this easy?
May this be washed in Lethe, and forgotten?

Chief Justice. I then did use the person of your father.
The image of his power lay then in me,
And, in the administration of his law,
Whiles I was busy for the commonwealth,
Your Highness pleased to forget my place,
The majesty and power of law and justice,
The image of the King whom I presented,
And struck me in my very seat of judgment,
Whereon, as an offender to your father,
I gave bold way to my authority
And did commit you.

Question your royal thoughts, make the
case yours,
Be now the father and propose a son,

120

Henry IV, Part II

Hear your own dignity so much profaned,
See your most dreadful laws so loosely slighted,
Behold yourself so by a son disdained,
And then imagine me taking your part
And in your power soft silencing your son.

After this cold considerance, sentence me.
And, as you are a king, speak in your state,
What I have done that misbecame my place,
My person, or my liege's sovereignty.

Hal's response, concerning Shakespeare's themes, may be the single most important speech in the *Henry IV* plays. The new King states,

You are right, Justice, and you weigh this well.
Therefore still bear the balance and the sword,
And I do wish your honors may increase,
Till you do live to see a son of mine
Offend you and obey you, as I did.
So shall I live to speak my father's words:
"Happy am I, that have a man so bold,
That dares do justice on my proper son,
And not less happy, having such a son,
That would deliver up his greatness so
Into the hands of justice."

There is my hand.
You shall be as a father to my youth.
My voice shall sound as you do prompt mine ear,
And I will stoop and humble my intents
To your well-practiced wise directions.

That is the thematic heart of the two *Henry IV* dramas, the playboy Prince -- after a riotous odyssey – grasping firmly the sceptre of law and justice. And, incidentally, discovering his true father.

> *King.* Now call we our high court of parliament.

With guiding advice from the Chief Justice, he will choose his counsellors and they will all prepare for the Coronation.

V.3   Gloucestershire. Shallow's orchard. Enter Falstaff, Shallow, Silence, Davy, Bardolph, and the Page.

> *Falstaff.* 'Fore God, you have here a goodly
>   dwelling and a rich.

> *Shallow.* Barren, barren, barren; beggars all,
>   beggars all, Sir John. Marry, good air.
>   Spread, Davy; spread, Davy. Well said, Davy.

Silence sings,

>   Do nothing but eat, and make good cheer,
>   And praise God for the merry year.

> *Falstaff.* There's a merry heart! Good Master
>   Silence, I'll give you a health for that anon.

> *Shallow.* Give Master Bardolph some wine, Davy.

And so, all of these singular characters, served by the precious Davy, do indeed make merry and hearty. To cap everything off, Pistol arrives with news from the Court, his entrance announced by Davy.

> *Falstaff.* From the Court! Let him come in.

Falstaff is fairly trembling with expectation, and Pistol is as excited as the gourmandising "man of war".

Pistol. Sir John, God save you.

He means "bless", not the modern apprehensive phrase.

Falstaff. What wind blew you hither, Pistol?

Pistol. Not the ill wind which blows no man to
good. Sweet knight, thou art now one of the
greatest men in this realm.

See what happens now:

Sir John, I am thy Pistol and thy friend,
And helter-skelter have I rode to thee,
And tidings do I bring and lucky joys
And golden times and happy news of price.

What happened? So joyous is the rough and crude Pistol
that he actually spoke in 10-syllable blank verse – **poetry.**

Falstaff. I pray thee now, deliver them like
a man of this world.

Pistol. Sir John, thy tender lambkin now is King.
Harry the Fifth's the man. I speak the truth.

Falstaff. What, is the old King dead?

Pistol. As nail in door. The things I speak are just.

Falstaff. Away, Bardolph! saddle my horse. Master
Robert Shallow, choose what office thou wilt in
the land, 'tis thine. Pistol, I will double-charge
thee with dignities.

Bardolph. O joyful day!
I would not take a knighthood for my fortune.

Falstaff. Carry Master Silence to bed.

The jolly Silence must have sung and drunk himself into unconsciousness. The overjoyed, bouncing Falstaff has more instructions:

> Master Shallow, my Lord Shallow--be what thou
> wilt, I am fortune's steward--get on thy boots.
> We'll ride all night. O sweet Pistol! Away,
> Bardolph!

Bardolph heads out.

> Boot, boot, Master Shallow. I know the young
> King is sick for me. Let us take any man's
> horses; the laws of England are at my commandment.

> Blessed are they that have been my friends, and
> woe to my Lord Chief Justice.

V.4   London: a street. Enter beadles (parish police) dragging in Mistress Quickly and Doll Tearsheet.

> *Doll.* Thou damned tripe-visaged rascal,
>   an the child I now go with do miscarry,
>   thou wert better thou hadst struck thy mother,
>   thou paper-faced villain.

> *Quickly.* O the Lord, that Sir John were come!
>   He would make this a bloody day to somebody.
>   But I pray God the fruit of her womb miscarry!

> *1st Beadle.* Come, I charge you both go with me;
>   for the man is dead that you and Pistol beat
>   amongst you.

> *Quickly.* O God, that right should thus overcome

might! Well, of sufferance comes ease.

If anything needs correction more than her morals, it is her malapropping abuse of the English language. (By the way, their punishment would probably be whipping.)

V.5 A public place near Westminster Abbey. The coronation will soon take place. Falstaff makes his entrance, along with Shallow, Pistol, Bardolph, and Falstaff's page.

> *Falstaff.* Stand here by me, Master Robert Shallow,
> I will make the King do you grace. I will leer
> upon him as 'a comes by. And do but mark the
> countenance that he will give me.
>
> *Pistol.* God bless thy lungs, good knight.
>
> *Falstaff.* Come here, Pistol, stand behind me.
> [*to Shallow*] O, if I had had time to have made
> new liveries, I would have bestowed the
> thousand pound I borrowed of you.

A thousand pounds drifts through our plays – the thousand pound Falstaff seized at Gad's Hill which Hal and Poins then seized away from him; the thousand-pound loan the Chief Justice abruptly refused him; and now the very same amount "borrowed" from the expectant, good-natured and excellently eccentric Justice Shallow. The thousand pounds amounts to a motif, telling an important part of the *Henry IV* saga, we might say, in sum.

> *Pistol.* My knight, I will inflame thy noble liver,
> And make thee rage.

> Thy Doll, and Helen of thy noble thoughts,
> Is in base durance and contagious prison.

Falstaff. I will deliver her.

Shouts are heard, and the sound of trumpets. The King and his train enter, the Lord Chief Justice amongst them.

> *Falstaff.* God save thy Grace, King Hal! my
> royal Hal!

> *Pistol.* The heavens thee guard and keep, most
> royal imp of fame!

> *Falstaff.* God save thee, my sweet boy!

The King hears this and says,

> My Lord Chief Justice, speak to that vain man.

> *Chief Justice (to Falstaff).* Have you your wits?
> Know you what 'tis you speak?

> *Falstaff.* My King! My Jove! I speak to thee,
> my heart!

> *King.* I know thee not, old man. Fall to thy prayers.
> How ill white hairs become a fool and jester!
> I have long dreamed of such a kind of man,
> So surfeit-swelled, so old, and so profane.
> But, being awaked, I do despise my dream.
>
> Make less thy body hence, and more thy grace.
> Leave gourmandising. Know the grave doth gape
> For thee thrice wider than for other men.

Hal anticipates a Falstaffian riposte here, for he says,

> Reply not to me with a fool-born jest.

Presume not that I am the thing I was,
For God doth know, so shall the world perceive,
That I have turned away my former self.
So will I those who kept me company.

When thou dost hear I am as I have been,
Approach me, and thou shalt be as thou wast,
The tutor and feeder of my riots.

Till then, I banish thee, on pain of death,
As I have done the rest of my misleaders,
Not to come near our person by ten mile.
For competence of life I will allow you,
That lack of means enforce you not to evil.
And, as we hear you do reform yourselves,
We will, according to your strengths and
    qualities,
Give you advancement.
Set on.   [*exeunt King and train*

Falstaff.   Master Shallow, I owe you a thousand
    pound.

Shallow.   Yea, marry, Sir John, which I beseech you
    to let me have home with me.

Falstaff.   That can hardly be, Master Shallow.
    Do not you grieve at this. I shall be sent for
    in private to him. Look you, he must seem thus
    to the world. Fear not your advancements. I
    will be the man yet that shall make you great.

Shallow.   I cannot well perceive how, unless you
    should give me your doublet and stuff me out
    with straw. I beseech you, good Sir John, let

me have five hundred of my thousand.

Falstaff. Go with me to dinner. Come, Lieutenant
Pistol; come, Bardolph. I shall be sent for
soon at night.

The Lord Chief Justice, Prince John, and officers come back
into the scene. The Chief Justice has something to say to
the officers:

Go, carry John Falstaff to the Fleet.
[The Fleet is a prison.]
Take all his company along with him.

Falstaff. My lord, my lord.

Chief Justice. I cannot now speak. I will
hear you soon.
Take them away.

Prince John. I like this fair proceeding
of the King's.
He hath intent his wonted followers
Shall all be very well provided for.
But all are banished till their conversations
Appear more wise and modest to the world.

And so it goes. Falstaff is on his way to prison, which
was probably inevitable given his presumption.

Note, however, that the Fleet in those days was not such
a bad place to reside for a while. It was intended for
upperclassmen who offended, was not altogether uncomfort-
table a lodging, and was primarily designed for questioning
and scolding. We can rest more-or-less assured that Falstaff
would be read a few lessons there, then released and granted
a modest pension, to be spent, of course, at least 10 miles

away from the King. This situation to last for a while, until his presumption diminished, presumably.

But his days as tutor and feeder of Hal's riots are over. The newly-crowned King prefers good governance to Falstaff, whatever the disgruntled comments of legions of Falstaff-lovers.

The Epilogue to *Henry IV, Part II* has us look forward to another play, *Henry V*, and mentions the Fleet's ponderous inmate:

> One word more, I beseech you. If you be not
> much cloyed with fat meat, our humble author
> will continue the story, with Sir John in it,
> and make you merry with fair Katharine of
> France; where, for anything I know, Falstaff shall
> die of a sweat, unless already 'a be killed with
> your hard opinions.

It is not **our** hard opinions which threaten Falstaff, Mr. Shakespeare. Most of us are too funloving to pose a dire threat to that outrageous man.

Shakespeare-in-Essence: The Adventures of Falstaff

Appendix to the Henry IV Chronicle Plays:
Two Notes on Falstaff

Shakespeare-in-Essence: The Adventures of Falstaff

1. Falstaff's undoing comes from **presumption**. Whenever he spoke with the Chief Justice, he sounded this note. (Worse, it was impudence and effrontery.) He took that pitch at other times with regard to the Prince, well before the final scene. When he said, "Let us take any man's horses; the laws of England are at my **commandment**" (my emphasis, and Shakespeare's via biblical usage), the bell rang loud-and-clear signalling his rather harsh Rejection.

I am much tempted to believe that Shakespeare was thinking of **hubris** when he nailed Falstaff in this way. **Hubris**, the classical Greek term for excessive pride, played an important part in Greek Tragedy. When the gods heard a mere mortal sounding his high proud presumption, they taught him -- or his survivors -- humility.

2. I fear to acquaint you with an unpleasant fact, one I still accept with difficulty. Shakespeare kills off Falstaff in *Henry V*, the successor drama to *Henry IV, Part II*. And Falstaff is given no lines to speak.

Furthermore, we learn from Pistol (Act II, scene 1, 118-128) that Falstaff dies of a broken heart, the result of his rejection (formally called in Shakespearean criticism, the Rejection of Falstaff).

Here is the dialogue, one of two instances in which *Henry V* refers to Falstaff.

> *Hostess Quickly.* As ever you came of women,
> come in quickly to Sir John. Ah, poor heart!
> He is so shaked of a burning quotidian tertian
> that it is most lamentable to behold. Sweet
> men, come to him.

Nym.   The King hath run bad humors on the knight;
   that's the even of it.

Pistol.   Nym, thou hast spoke the right.
   His heart is fracted and corroborate.

Whatever the precise linguistic sources of his malapropping language, he means broken.

By way of compensation, however, the dramatist does the mortifying deed by associating Falstaff with the immortal Socrates. The connection is not altogether illogical.

Both were gadflies, although of very different qualities. Socrates stood for virtue, even upon pain of death. No stretch of the imagination can bring Falstaff within this ambit. But fundamentally, each sorely questioned conventional values, stimulating his audience to analyze, to look beneath the surface, to question assumptions. Falstaff does this with his life-style and, particularly, his marvellous Honor-speech on the battlefield of *Part I*.

I surmise that Shakespeare was already thinking of Socrates when in *Part I* the Prince, playing his father during the skit, refers to Falstaff as "that villanous abominable **misleader of youth**" (my emphasis). This echoes in *Part II* when the Chief Justice accuses Falstaff,

You have misled the youthful prince.

The phrase and notion resonates again when King Henry V denounces Falstaff as a "misleader" and "the tutor and feeder of my riots". These true statements sound like accusations levelled against Socrates, that of corrupting youth.

I quote from *Henry V* the obvious parody of the death of Socrates in Plato's *Phaedo*. Shakespeare almost repeats Plato, except for the risqué humor of his rendition.

Act II, scene 3. London, the Hostess' house in Eastcheap.

> *Hostess.* 'a [he] parted even just between twelve and one, even at the turning o' the tide: for after I saw him smile upon his fingers' ends, I knew there was but one way; [not yet the parody] for his nose was as sharp as a pen, and 'a babbled of green fields. **How now, Sir John!** quoth I, **what, man! be o' good cheer.** So 'a cried out – **God, God, God!** three or four times. Now I, to comfort him, bid him **'a should not think of God; I hoped there was no need to trouble himself with any such thoughts yet.** [that's a jest, meaning that he will be punished by God for the way he has lived; now comes the parody of Plato]
> So 'a bade me lay more clothes on his feet.
> I put my hand into the bed and felt them, and they were as cold as any stone; then I felt to his knees, and so upward and upward, and all was as cold as any stone.

Almost identical was the test to note the hemlock's progress on the Athenian philosopher.

Risqúe humor mimicking the death of Socrates – Falstaff would have liked it that way.

Shakespeare-in-Essence: The Adventures of Falstaff

The Merry Wives of Windsor

Falstaff in love and farce

"I do mean to make love to Ford's wife."

Falstaff

The Merry Wives of Windsor

Tradition has it that Queen Elizabeth, smitten with Falstaff from the *Henry IV* dramas, commanded Shakespeare to write a play about Falstaff in love. The legend has not only appeal but the appearance of verity.

Shakespeare composed *The Merry Wives of Windsor* around the great round rogue, victimizing the blustering braggart and thwarting his every licentious and pecuniary desire. Critics unsympathetically find poor corpulent Falstaff a slender shadow of his former self. But the comedy is merry and brisk, and I consider Falstaff greater than ever for his grace in defeat. Besides, did not the man say of himself,

> I am not only witty in myself,
> but the cause that wit is in other men.
> [and *women*, as we shall see]

So his role in this very English locale and farce keeps him in character, and gives us some jolly fun. That, I maintain, does Falstaff proud.

Briefly let me mention another legend, that Shakespeare as a youth stole a deer from a local landowner's preserve. An exchange in the first scene brings it to mind:

> *Falstaff.* Now, Master Shallow, you'll complain of me to the king?

> *Shallow.* Knight, you have beaten my men, killed my deer, and broke open my lodge.

> *Falstaff.* But not kiss'd your keeper's daughter?

So much for hearsay. To deal with the more concrete, Shakespeare spices up an already tasty endeavor with a variety of humorous accents and linguistic indiscretions. To wit,

Slender. I will marry her, sir, at your request. But if
there be no great love in the beginning, yet
heaven may decrease it upon better
acquaintance, when we are married and have
more occasion to know one another. I hope,
upon familiarity will grow more contempt.
But if you say, 'marry her,' I will marry her;
that I am freely dissolved, and dissolutely.

Slender practices "malapropism". Parson Evans answers
him, employing his native Welsh dialect:

It is a fery discretion answer; save the faul
is in the ort 'dissolutely'. The ort is,
according to our meaning, 'resolutely'
-- his meaning is goot.

One must expect these kinds of things to pervade a
Shakespearean Englishy burlesque.

Act I, scene 3.   The plot begins to unfold with Falstaff,
not malapropriately, drinking in a tavern. His men Pistol,
Nym, and Bardolph hear him apprise the host of the Garter
Inn,

Falstaff. I must turn away some of my followers.

He tells them directly,

I am almost out at heels.
There is no remedy.
I must cony-catch, I must shift.

Our slang word, to "con", has a lineal descent from "cony-
catch", to catch a gull, trick, defraud. Robert Greene wrote
a series of interesting pamphlets on the art.

Falstaff explains how he will shift:

> I do mean to make love to Ford's wife.
> [Ford, a respectable citizen of Windsor]
> I spy entertainment in her; she discourses,
> she carves, she gives the leer of invitation.
> I can construe the action of her familiar
> style; and the hardest voice of her behavior,
> to be English'd rightly, is, 'I am Sir John
> Falstaff's.'
>
> Now, the report goes she has all the rule of
> her husband's purse -- he hath a legion of
> angels [coins bearing the figure of an angel
> stamped in gold].
>
> I have writ me here a letter to her; and have
> another to Page's wife, [she, another respectable
>   lady married to a respectable citizen]
> who even now gave me good eyes too, examined
> my parts with most judicious oeillades; sometimes
> the beam of her view idled my foot, sometimes my
> portly belly.

Pistol (aside to Nym). Then did the sun on dunghill shine.

Nym (aside to Pistol).   I thank thee for that humor.

Falstaff.   O, she did so course o'er my exteriors with
   such a greedy intention, that the appetite of her
   eye did seem to scorch me up like a burning-glass!
   Here's another letter to her; she bears the purse
   too; she is a region in Guiana, all gold and
   bounty. I will be cheaters to them both, and
   they shall be exchequers to me. They shall be

> my East and West Indies, and I will trade
>   to them both.
> Go bear thou this letter to Mistress Page; and
> thou this to Mistress Ford. We will thrive,
>   lads, we will thrive.

Pistol and Nym refuse to carry a letter, and the two missives are given to the page, Robin. Nym and Pistol do not trust Falstaff to provide for them. Angry at having been turned out, Nym will inform Page, and Pistol likewise to Ford, what Falstaff is up to with their wives and money.

Act II, scene 1.   Mistress Page and Mistress Ford are friends. Upon receiving Falstaff's love letters, they tell one another and compare communiques -- which happen to be exactly the same.

> *Mistress Page.*   Let's consult together against this
>   greasy knight.

They will conspire to discomfit said "greasy knight". Meanwhile, Pistol and Nym acquaint the ladies' husbands with Falstaff's nefarious designs. If Pistol had any qualms about sabotaging Falstaff, their next meeting in the tavern dispels them.

II.2

> *Falstaff.* I will not lend thee a penny.

> *Pistol.* Why, then the world's mine oyster,
>   Which I with sword will open.

> *Falstaff.* Not a penny.

The Merry Wives of Windsor

Mistress Ford sends a cony-catching message to Falstaff, that he should come to her house between 10 and 11 in the morning when her husband will be away. Mistress Page also commends herself to the knight: her husband is seldom from home, but she hopes there will come a time . . .

Ford, one of the intended cuckolds, comes to see Falstaff. He impersonates a "Master Brook" and sends ahead of him "a morning's draught of sack" to soften up Falstaff for his trickery. Ford ("Brook") enters, places a bag of money on the table in front of Falstaff, and tells the avid gentleman to help himself to its contents. This represents payment for a favor. What is it? "Brook" wants Falstaff to sleep with Ford's wife. He asks the already designing rogue "to lay an amiable siege to her honesty"; in short, to seduce her.

> *Ford.* I could drive her then from the ward of her
> purity, her reputation, her marriage-vow, and a
> thousand other her defences, which now are
> too-too strongly embattled against me.
> What say you to 't, Sir John?

> *Falstaff* (*weighing the bag in his hand*). Master Brook,
> I will first make bold with your money; next,
> give me your hand; and last, as I am a gentleman,
> you shall, if you will, enjoy Ford's wife.

He reveals his plan to Ford:

> I shall be with her – I may tell you – by her own
> appointment. Even as you came in to me, her
> assistant, or go-between [Mistress Quickly],
> parted from me. I say I shall be with her
> between ten and eleven; for at that time the

jealous rascally knave, her husband, will be
forth. Come you to me at night; you shall
know how I speed.

Ford. I am blest in your acquaintance. Do you know
Ford, sir?

Falstaff. Hang him, poor cuckoldy knave! I know
him not – yet I wrong him to call him poor.
They say the jealous wittolly knave hath
masses of money; for the which his wife
seems to me well-favor'd. I will use her as
the key of the cuckoldy rogue's coffer; and
there's my harvest-home.

Ford. I would you knew Ford, sir, that you might
avoid him, if you saw him.

Falstaff. Hang him, mechanical salt-butter rogue!
I will stare him out of his wits; I will awe him
with my cudgel -- it shall hang like a meteor
o'er the cuckold's horns.

A husband whose wife cheated on him -- a cuckold -- was
said to have horns on his head.

Master Brook, thou shalt know I will predominate
over the peasant, and thou shalt lie with his wife.
Come to me soon at night. Ford's a knave, and I
will aggravate his style. Thou, Master Brook,
shalt know him for knave and cuckold.

[*exit*

Ford, alone, furious:

Cuckold! The devil himself hath not such a
name. Page is an ass, a secure ass; he will

trust his wife; he will not be jealous. I will rather trust a Fleming with my butter, Parson Hugh the Welshman with my cheese, an Irishman with my aqua-vitae bottle, or a thief to walk my ambling gelding, than my wife with herself.

Eleven o'clock the hour! I will prevent this, detect my wife, be revenged on Falstaff, and laugh at Page. I will about it; better three hours too soon than a minute too late. Fie, fie, fie! cuckold! cuckold! cuckold!

He rushes out of the room.

Act III, scene 3. The hall of Master Ford's house. Falstaff enters it.

Falstaff (to Mistress Ford). Now let me die ("die", slang for sexual climax, satisfaction), for I have lived long enough. This is the period of my ambition. O blessed hour!

Mistress Ford. O sweet Sir John!

Before Falstaff can get down to business, his page Robin calls from without:

Robin. Mistress Ford, Mistress Ford! Here's Mistress Page at the door, sweating, and blowing, and looking wildly, and would needs speak with you presently.

Falstaff. She shall not see me. I will ensconce me behind the arras.

Mistress Ford. Pray you, do so. She's a very tattling
woman.

Of course, Mistresses Ford and Page share each other's
confidence. But what Mistress Page hastens to communicate
will come as a surprise to everyone.

Enter Mistress Page and Robin
Falstaff hides behind the tapestry

Mistress Ford. What's the matter, good Mistress Page?

Mistress Page. O well-a-day, Mistress Ford! Having
an honest man to your husband, to give him
such cause of suspicion.

Mistress Ford. Why, alas, what's the matter?

Mistress Page. Your husband's coming hither,
woman, with all the officers in Windsor, to
search for a gentleman that he says is here
now in the house, by your consent, to take an
ill advantage of his absence. You are undone.

Mistress Ford. 'Tis not so, I hope.

But 'tis so, and they must scramble. Mistress Page points
out a large basket and suggests the gentleman may step in,
be covered with dirty linen, and carried out by two servants.

Mistress Ford. He's too big to go in there.
What shall I do?

But Falstaff will take any chance of escape. He thrusts the
arras aside and rushes towards the basket.

Falstaff. Let me see't, let me see't, O, let me see't!
I'll in, I'll in. Follow your friend's counsel.

146

Mistress Page. What, Sir John Falstaff! Are these your
letters, knight?

Falstaff (aside to Mistress Page). I love thee, and none
but thee. [*aloud*] Help me away. Let me creep
in here.

Falstaff struggles into the basket and they cover him with
foul laundry. Just then Master Ford and others enter the
house in search of Falstaff (recall that Falstaff had told him,
"Brook", when and where he would be). The servants
manage to get this terribly heavy basket past them, carrying
it to the Thames river into which they dump foul linen and
Falstaff.

Ford, disappointed in his pursuit, wonders if "the knave
bragged of that he could not compass". Aside, Mrs. Ford
says to her friend Mrs. Page,

> Shall we send that foolish carrion, Mistress
> Quickly, to him [Falstaff], and excuse his
> throwing into the water; and give him another
> hope, to betray him to another punishment?

The two merry wives of Windsor decide that they shall.

III. 5   The confounded Ford, disguised again as Brook,
visits Falstaff who relates his debacle. He tells of Ford's
entering the house in angry quest of his wife's lover.

Ford.   What! while you were there?

Falstaff. While I was there.

Ford.   And did he search for you, and could not
find you?

Falstaff. You shall hear. As good luck would have it,

comes in one Mistress Page; gives intelligence
of Ford's approach; and, in her invention and
Ford's wife's distraction, they convey'd me
into a buck-basket.

Ford.   A buck-basket!

Falstaff. By the Lord, a buck-basket! – ramm'd me in
with foul shirts and smocks, socks, foul
stockings, greasy napkins; that, Master
Brook, there was the rankest compound of
villainous smell that ever offended nostril.

Ford.   And how long lay you there?

Falstaff. Nay, you shall hear, Master Brook, what I
have suffer'd to bring this woman to evil for
your own good.
     Being thus cramm'd in the basket, a
couple of Ford's knaves, his hinds, were
call'd forth by their mistress to carry me in
the name of foul clothes to Datchet-lane.
They took me on their shoulders; met the
jealous knave their master in the door, who
asked them once or twice what they had in
their basket. I quaked for fear, lest the
lunatic knave would have search'd it. But
fate, ordaining he should be a cuckold, held
his hand.

Falstaff recounts also the immense physical discomforts
attendant upon his misadventure. He was situated in the
basket,

hilt to point, heel to head; and then
to be stopt in, like a strong distillation,

with stinking clothes that fretted in their own
grease. Think of that, a man of my kidney!
think of that -- it was a miracle to scape
suffocation.

   And in the height of this bath, when I
was more than half stew'd in grease, like a
Dutch dish, to be thrown into the Thames,
and cool'd, glowing hot, in that surge, like
a horseshoe!

The awful story told, Falstaff discloses information of
another assignation:

   Her husband is this morning gone a-birding.
   I have received from her another embassy of
   meeting; 'twixt eight and nine is the hour,
   Master Brook.

Ford.   'Tis past eight already, sir.

Falstaff. Is it? I will then address me to my
   appointment. Come to me at your convenient
   leisure, and you shall know how I speed; and
   the conclusion shall be crown'd with your
   enjoying her. Adieu. Master Brook, you
   shall cuckold Ford.   [*he goes*

Ford (solo). Hum, ha! Is this a vision? Is this a dream?
   Do I sleep? Master Ford, awake! awake,
   Master Ford! there's a hole in your best coat,
   Master Ford. This 'tis to be married! this
   'tis to have linen and buck-baskets!

   I will now take the lecher. He is at my
   house; he cannot scape me.

He rushes out.

Act IV, scene 1.   Enter Mistress Page, her schoolboy son William, and the daffy servant to a Doctor Caius, Mistress Quickly. Parson Evans, he of the Welsh accent, arrives to quiz William on his Latin lessons.

> *Evans.*   I pray you, have your remembrance, child; *accusativo, hung, hang, hog.*

> *Mistress Quickly.* Hang-hog is Latin for bacon, I warrant you.

> *Evans.* Leave your prabbles, oman. What is the focative case, William?

> *William.* O, -- *vocativo*, O.

> *Evans.* Remember, William; focative is *caret.*

> *Mistress Quickly.* And that's a good root.

(Is there perhaps method to her madness?)

> *Evans.* Oman, forbear.

> *Mistress Page.* Peace!

> *Evans.* What is your genitive case plural, William?

> *William.* Genitive case!

> *Evans.* Ay.

> *William. Genitivo,* -- *horum, harum, horum.*

In case the reader might miss the last one, the playwright has Mistress Quickly quickly say,

> Vengeance of Jenny's case! Fie on her!
> Never name her, child, if she be a whore.

(Ipso facto, "whore 'em, harem, whore 'em")

Evans. Show me now, William, some declensions of
   your pronouns.

William. Forsooth, I have forgot.

Possibly you have fathomed who little William happens to
be. If not, let me do an Evans and ask you a question. Do
you have your remembrance of Shakespeare's first name?

IV.2   The hall in Master Ford's house; the buck-basket
in a corner. Falstaff and Mistress Ford are together. As
Falstaff warms to the occasion, again Mistress Page comes
a-shouting that Ford returns – this time with his brothers
who are armed with pistols. The wives Ford and Page shunt
Falstaff upstairs to dress in the garb of the old woman of
Brainford, the aunt of a maid, a "witch", husband Ford calls
her.

   Ford, choking with anger, enters and goes instantly for
the basket to nab Falstaff. But the bloated rascal lies not
within. Soon, Falstaff descends the stairs in woman's
clothing, which Ford recognizes. He beats 'her', "you witch,
you rag, you baggage". After a good cudgeling, Falstaff
escapes into the street.

   The merry wives decide to tell their husbands all. And
they will devise one additional sport at "this old fat
fellow's" expense.

IV.4   A room in Ford's house. Both wives with their
husbands, and Hugh Evans.

Mistress Page. There is an old tale goes that

Herne the hunter,
Sometime a keeper here in Windsor forest,
Doth all the winter-time, at still midnight,
Walk round about an oak, with great ragg'd
    horns.
And there he blasts the tree, and takes the cattle,
. . . and shakes a chain
In a most hideous and dreadful manner.
You have heard of such a spirit, and well you
    know
The superstitious idle-headed eld
Received, and did deliver to our age,
This tale of Herne the Hunter for a truth.

They will have Falstaff, disguised like Herne, with huge
horns on his head, meet them in the park at midnight by a
particular oak tree. Children dressed as fairies will encircle
him, pinching and burning him with tapers.

Act V, scene 1. Mistress Quickly again acts as messenger,
conveying to Falstaff information about the latest liaison.

> *Falstaff.* This is the third time. I hope good luck
> lies in odd numbers.

V.5   Falstaff appears beneath a mighty oak in Windsor
Park, disguised as Herne the Hunter, wearing a buck's head.

> *Falstaff.* The Windsor bell hath struck twelve; the
> minute draws on. Now, the hot-blooded gods
> assist me!

152

The two merry wives come to him, and he thinks to have them both. The "fairies" noise their approach, the women run away, and the little demons torment poor Falstaff with pinching and burning. He pulls off the buck's head, and would escape, but the Fords and Pages confront him.

The irony that he, *Falstaff*, wears the horns, not Ford and Page, dawns on him. They explain everything, and Falstaff takes it like a frustrated but good sport.

Mistress Page. Good husband, let us every one go home,
    And laugh this sport o'er by a country fire,
    Sir John and all.

Ford. Let it be so. Sir John,
    To Master Brook you yet shall hold your word,
    For he tonight shall lie with Mistress Ford.

[*exeunt*

Finis

Index

of Characters Appearing
in this In-Essence rendition
of the plays

Henry IV, Part I
Falstaff
Prince Henry (Hal), heir
  to the throne of England
Hotspur, the brilliant rebel
King Henry IV (the former
  Bolingbroke, usurper of
  the English throne from
  Richard II)

Bardolph, a crony of
  Falstaff and Hal
Douglas, Earl of, a great
  fighting Scotsman
Francis, a waiter in the
  Boar's Head Tavern in
  Eastcheap
Gadshill, a setter (arranger
  of robberies)
Glendower, Owen
  leader of Welsh rebels
Hostess Quickly, of the
  Boar's Head

John of Lancaster, prince
  and younger brother to
  Hal
Kate (Lady Percy,
  Hotspur's wife)
Mortimer, named heir by
  Richard II, rebel against
  Henry IV
Northumberland, an earl
  and a great magnate,
  father of Hotspur
Peto, crony of Falstaff
Poins, a highborn crony of
  Hal and Falstaff, unlike
  Bardolph and Peto
Vernon, Sir Richard
Vintner, of the Boar's
  Head
Worcester, an earl and
  member of the
  Northumberland party

Henry IV, Part II
Falstaff
Prince Henry (becoming
King Henry V)
Prince John (of Lancaster)
younger brother of Prince
Henry
King Henry IV
Lord Chief Justice

Archbishop, of York
Bardolph (Falstaff's
crony)
Bardolph, Lord (ally of
Northumberland)
beadles (parish police)
Bullcalf, an unwilling
recruit
Clarence, Thomas of (one
of the princely brothers)
Coleville, a rebel knight
Doll Tearsheet, a wanton
of the Boar's Head
Tavern and girl friend
of Falstaff
Fang, an officer
Feeble, a recruit
Hastings, a lord in
opposition to the King
Gloucester, Humphrey of
(another of the princely
brothers)

Lady Percy, the deceased
Hotspur's wife Kate
Morton, associate of
Northumberland
Mouldy, as unwilling a
recruit as Bullcalf
Mowbray, a lord in
opposition to the King,
son of the Mowbray in
Richard II
Northumberland, Earl of
Peto and Pistol, cronies
of Falstaff
Poins, crony of Prince
Henry and Falstaff
Quickly, Mistress
(Hostess of the
Boar's Head Tavern)
Rumor
Servant, of the Chief
Justice
Shadow, a recruit
Shallow, a country justice
Silence, a country justice
Snare, an officer
Travers, a lord in
opposition to the King
Wart, a recruit
Warwick, an earl of the
King's party
Westmoreland, an earl of
the King's party

Index

R

redeem, redemption, 21,
24, 25, 84
reformed, 57
rejection (of Falstaff), 133
riot(s), riotous, 14, 114,
127, 129, 134

S

sack, 9, 14, 15, 37, 38, 45,
56, 59, 65, 83, 85, 87,
109, 143

T

thousand pound(s), 38,
39, 77, 125, 127

V

vain, vanity, 47, 58, 84,
113, 126

The Merry Wives of Windsor

Falstaff
Mistress Ford, a merry
  wife of Windsor
Mistress Page, a merry
  wife of Windsor
Master Ford, an intended
  cuckold
Master Page, an intended
  cuckold
Mistress Quickly, a
  go-between
Nym, a crony of Falstaff
Parson Evans, a hasher
  of the English language
Pistol, a crony of Falstaff
Robin, a page of Falstaff
Slender, a practioner of
  malapropism
Shallow, a country justice
William, a lad struggling
  futilely with Latin

Printed in the United States
21125LVS00002B/112-126